POWER AND INFLUENCE

Through

PUBLIC SPEAKING

POWER AND

INFLUENCE THROUGH PUBLIC SPEAKING

Cy Campbell

Parker Publishing Company, Inc.
West Nyack, New York

Library of Congress Cataloging in Publication Data

Campbell, Cy, date
    Power and influence through public speaking.

    1. Public speaking. 2. Persuasion (Rhetoric)
I. Title.
PN4121.C227   808.5'1   72-5960
ISBN 0-13-686949-1

Printed in the United States of America

DEDICATION

To my family:

My parents and my brothers, Russell and Vernon, who
started me on the road to effective communication

My wife Marge who joined me on the journey

My sons Bruce and Kurt who are encouraged to travel
further

HOW THIS BOOK WILL INCREASE
YOUR POWER
AND INFLUENCE

You, too, can influence others by public speaking. Whether you number your audience in the hundreds or chat with a limited few, the basic principles of communication are the same.

What do we mean by *influence?* To influence is to produce an effect without apparent force or direct authority, to persuade listeners to perform actions or understand reasons behind actions.

From our earliest days, we have been influenced by those around us, consciously or unconsciously. There are practical, proven ways to influence others. Those who use them are called *leaders.* Why not be a leader?

Learn the rules. Practice them daily. Eventually, they will be part of you. Ignorance is a voluntary misfortune. If you have not understood or discovered that public speaking can be comfortable, even enjoyable, now is the time to think about it.

Your ideas are valuable. Loyalty to your family, your job, your community demands that you share your considered thoughts, present your answers to problems that are frightening people today. If you do have ideas, you can stimulate others to action through speech.

Leadership is not pre-designated for specific individuals. Leadership comes from within, from self-confidence. Build your own self-image by knowing the rules. Recognize your worth. Let others gain from your abilities.

Never before has any civilization been so articulate. Never before have so many asked questions. Never before have the problems been of such universal concern.

But time is vital. No one listens at a leisurely pace. Even television devotees are expected to concentrate only for limited periods. At one time, orators were judged by length as well as content. In Cotton Mather's ministry, sermons could be long. The congregation expected that. Today, there are more diversions, more claims upon a man's time. To be effective, sermons must be short and direct. Many well-known religious leaders restrict themselves to 20-minute sermons. One Navy chaplain said the sailors who listened to him at services they chose to attend, lost interest rapidly after nine minutes.

Physical strength was as important as brain power for centuries. William Jennings Bryan, the silver-tongued orator, when he campaigned for the Presidency, spoke as often as 36 times a day, releasing a torrent of 80,000 words. He could be heard by 50,000 people at a time—without the benefit of any amplifiers! One of his detractors, denying his integrity, declared his "patriotism was all in his jawbone." No doubt, other men cherished the same thoughts, but they could not compete with that magnificent sound box.

Today, the emphasis has shifted. No one needs lung power to sway the multitude. The accent is on brain power. But that power must extend to the presentation of the material as well as the content.

And make no mistake—just because your audience is limited, your influence is not. Of the hundreds who listen to any platform speaker, how many are stimulated? Your impact on an audience of four or five, multiplied 20 times as you go through the week, may be greater than that of the paid public performer; that is, if your ideas are worthwhile and if (a very large IF) you can present them understandably.

So what is public speaking? Public speaking is speaking to the public, no matter how many, at any specific time. Perhaps the value of this book lies in its explanation of logical, understandable patterns for communication. Maybe you have not realized the strength of the right word, the simple word.

You have recognized the value of a short, sharp blow in offensive fighting as against a steady, light pummeling. Have you ever related it to persuasive, action-demanding speech?

Varied types of speeches demand varied approaches. What stimulates a response from a group of businessmen snatching a precious lunch hour together, will not be the right approach for a senior citizens' club that accepts a request from someone who wishes to gain their votes for a community project.

Where do speakers get their jokes? How can you be sure your statistics are adequate or even accurate? This manual will give you an introduction to the world of research, to a practical way of storing or finding humor for possible future use. People listen four times as fast as you can speak. Are you giving them enough material to keep their attention focussed on the subject?

Participation—if only mentally—will hold your audience. A laugh is a physical activity, and in that alone, is helpful. It can awaken a sluggish individual who mistakenly believes that listening is a passive activity.

We are all involved in a civilization that is straining forward so rapidly that people cannot wait to deliberate. They want action. They also want to be led in the right direction. We need responsible citizens who can communicate, who can carry the message clearly and concisely. Are you willing to be one of them?

Cy Campbell

ACKNOWLEDGMENTS

I am grateful for the collaboration of my wife Marjorie, a writer and public speaker herself, who has been researcher and secretary, spending often more time than I on gathering material from random notes I have kept over the years.

I am indebted, too, to Larry Sweeney, an effective platform speaker, leader, and instructor, and to Dorothy Jones and Eliza Jane Coronel, both creative writers of wit and imagination, who read the manuscript and alternately agreed and disagreed with my premises and my phrasing.

To Marcella Lawson who typed my manuscript, interpreting hieroglyphics, and carefully sorting out pages, I owe much.

I appreciate the cooperation of my employer, the San Diego Division of General Dynamics, who encouraged and sponsored my serving as an officer in national professional societies and permitted travelling to many conventions to deliver papers concerning our product.

ACKNOWLEDGMENTS

I am grateful, too, for the patience of hundreds of men who listened to and evaluated my speaking through the years in Toastmaster Club #457, District 5, and to all Toastmasters who gave me the opportunity to serve in local and international offices.

May you gain as much from reading this book as I have from writing it.

C.C.

Table of Contents

You Are Unique — You Are Not Unique — Communication
Is Vital — Make Your Subconscious Your Servant — Is
Silence Golden or Just Yellow?

Your Family Has to Listen — Your Co-Workers Have Ears
and Minds — Companies Spread Their Influence Through
Their Spokesmen — Communities on the Move Look for Leadership — Church Work Is a Challenge — The Wide, Wide World
Is Waiting for You.

One Man Leads to Many — Each Man Stands at the Center of
the Universe — Level with Your Listener — Some Listeners
Already Agree with You — Some Listeners Are Willing to Be
Convinced — Some Listeners Are Too Tired to Care — Some
Listeners Bring the Body but Turn Off the Ears — Some
Listeners Have Chips on Their Shoulders — This Above All.

Rude – Have You Really Made Your Point?

Your Timing Is Essential – When Information Is Your Only Goal – Action Is Wanted – Sharing an Experience – Inspiration Is the Target – Leave 'em Laughing – Finish with Strength – When You're Finished, Stop – Thank You - Never – In Capsule Form.

Section IV   PRESENTING YOUR SPEECH

Voice Tone Can Be Learned or Improved – Articulate with Precision – Pronounce Every Word Correctly – Pacing Is Pertinent – Pause for Understanding – Vary Your Volume and Stress – Dramatic Techniques Are Effective – Let Your Feelings Show – Should You Read? – But, Nevertheless.

Make Your First Impression Powerful – Stand at Ease – Look at Your Listeners – Handy Hints – From Honolulu to Rome, Body Talk Is Important – Match Action to Words – The Main Point.

Simple Words Are Always Preferable – Familiar Words Are More Meaningful – Accents Are Acceptable – Slang Is Unnecessary – Some Words Should Be Avoided – Be Original – Words Create Pictures, Moods, Emotions – Take a Positive Position.

Your Emotions and Opinions Add Color to Your Ideas – Concentrate on Your Listeners – You Are More Important than Your Clothes – Warmth and Enthusiasm Are More Stimulating than Perfection – Cultivate a Sense of Humor – Be

Subtle — Recognize Your Own Worth.

Humor Has Many Uses — Short Quips Evoke Interest — Obvious Exaggeration Delights Most Listeners — Anecdotes Are for Everyone — Parodies and Personal Limericks Please — Movement Adds Merriment — Good Jokes Are Like Good Music — Never, Never, Never — Research for Fun.

Answer Your Own Questions First — Questions from the Audience — What Have You Got to Say to That?

Before the Talk Begins — Don't Recognize Everyone — Apologize - Never! — Poetry Enriches — Visual Aids Clarify Ideas — Listening Needs Understanding — The Finished Speech.

Section V   SPEECH SITUATIONS

Telephones Reach Everywhere — Telephone Courtesy Is Important — Everyone Should Know How to Use a Tape Recorder — Some People Prefer Radio.

Guide a Group Effectively — Rules Establish Limits — Open the Meeting — Introduce a Speaker with Finesse — Buzz Sessions Involve the Members — Reports Must Be Useful and Clear — Salesmen Have a Special Approach.

Home-Town Conventions Are Great Opportunities — Conven-

POWER AND INFLUENCE

Through

PUBLIC SPEAKING

Section I

YOU AND YOUR
POTENTIAL AUDIENCE

1 You Can and Should Influence Others

YOU can be a leader. You can make your world a better place by influencing others more effectively. Your opinions and suggestions may make a vital difference. Change comes through communication. Most communication is oral. To make more changes, you have to communicate with more people. Public speaking can be your weapon of influence.

You can be successful in public speaking. You can put your ideas across with clarity and enthusiasm. With understanding, you can forget yourself, as you lead your listeners to new channels of thought and action.

Are you afraid to speak before others? Do you feel your opinion is unimportant? Are you certain that what you think has already been considered and discarded by the "brains"?

Gaps of understanding and experience separate all of us. The man who can build bridges over these gaps is not always the most educated or the most skillful in speaking. The man who sees and understands may be you. You are the one needed to introduce new ideas or to keep the path of communication clear and open between different cultures and ideas.

How can you accomplish this? Read this book. Accept its principles and you will have the keys to unlock your personality and your opinions, to overcome fear and build self-confidence. Your reputation among your colleagues will rise. You will begin the climb to leadership in every phase of your life. Your influence will be automatic.

Why wait until tomorrow? Begin today.

YOU ARE UNIQUE

Have you ever considered that you are the only one with your particular background? Even Siamese twins view the world from different perspectives. How much more individuality you can bring to any subject by your particular slant, based on that special frame of reference that has been building itself as a honeycomb around you.

Perceptive, searching listeners are anxious to hear what you have to say. And you owe it—not only to yourself, but also to those around you—to give a balanced opinion on movements of the day. Thus comes progress of the kind that you want, that businessmen, statesmen, parents, and leaders everywhere need to build a better world.

You and you only fit into a particular niche in your company. You are not paid to occupy space, to keep your thoughts to yourself. Your employer needs to know. Can you afford to let him down—to let yourself down? How can he know your abilities unless you speak out?

YOU ARE NOT UNIQUE

Are you afraid that you are the only tongue-tied man of

your acquaintance—that all great leaders were born with the gift of ready, persuasive speech? Not so! From earliest recorded history, men have feared their inadequacy in speech.

More than 3,000 years ago, one young man, fearful of his success, cried, "I am not eloquent . . . I am slow of speech and of tongue . . . send, I pray some other person" (*Exodus* 4:10).

But Moses was not excused. His message was urgent. Other more fluent speakers did not feel strongly enough, so Moses forgot himself in his concern for his people, and eventually, Pharaoh listened.

Throughout history, men have overcome their weaknesses, their timidity and risen to leadership, once they have acknowledged the ability within them waiting to be released. Some, like Demosthenes, are legends. He studied the elements of communication and practiced alone, for his defects were many. He had so much to say, but people laughed at his mannerisms, his voice, his appearance.

You have much more to help you, with modern mechanical advances. But even as before, with understanding and desire, you can master public speaking techniques that are elementary. Once they are buried in your subconscious, you can advance to the vital core of your speech—your ideas.

Join the thinkers. Prepare yourself for easy communication with those around you. Prepare yourself for leadership by learning the rules.

COMMUNICATION IS VITAL

From sages to streetsweepers, we all deplore the generation gap, the political gap, the racial gap. Can you personally close the gap? Not likely. But words carefully chosen can build bridges, and really, why should we close any gap? Progress comes by leaps. We must not lose touch or understanding with each other. We must communicate.

No one culture is complete unto itself. Adaptations

from other generations, from other races, from other political systems will strengthen or add meaning to our own way of life.

You can help by being a bridge-builder. Expensive educations and unlimited vocabularies are not assurance that the possessor has insight into problems. Why depend upon a word expert? Jump in yourself. Offer your experienced analysis of the doubtful situation. Offer your solution. If you can suggest something worthwhile, your ability will be recognized. Your influence will be felt.

Because someone else is more at ease in speaking, because another man has a recognized high intelligence, don't hesitate. No man can encompass all fields of knowledge. A really intelligent man realizes this and welcomes interpretation by others who are closer to or more aware of specific problems and their possible solutions. You are, of necessity, the bridge-builder between the problem and its successful outcome.

What kind of bridge will you build? Across a simple stream, a rough plank will suffice. Everyone knows why his support is wanted for the annual Red Cross fund drive. A canvasser needs only a sentence to request a contribution. As the gap widens, the gap of understanding, your structure or bridge, requires greater reinforcement. In what way does a man gain if the bond drive for better schools passes? If he has no children and a fixed income, he needs a fuller explanation, a thought-out, well-expressed summary of benefits. You will have to build well to carry him across to full understanding.

Practice is not enough. Practice does not "make perfect." Practice, without realizing or using the established working rules for persuasion or clear explanation, leads only to strengthening habits that may be undesirable and fall short of accomplishing your purpose.

You may already be a "rough diamond," but polishing or cutting away needless material will increase the value of your speech, letting the true radiance shine. Once you have mastered the fundamental rules of communicating clearly, you can go one step further. You can influence those around you to believe as you do, to vote, or to support those people or groups whom you recognize as worthwhile.

MAKE YOUR SUBCONSCIOUS YOUR SERVANT

First of all, make your subconscious your servant. How? Easy! Learn the rules of public speaking. Try them out, thinking about them consciously—one rule at a time—as you read through the following pages. By use, by conscious thought, they will supplant those chance-begotten speaking habits you have developed without awareness throughout the years. Your subconscious can be taught; it can even be retaught to overcome inefficient or automatic reactions. Old dogs frequently learn new tricks, but it takes thought and more effort. The results are worth the struggle. Good speech habits can become as involuntary and simple as yesterday's solved problems look today.

Eventually, the new techniques will become so much a part of you through your subconscious that you will be able to concentrate on your ideas. For let us never forget that your ideas are the valuable part of your communicating.

How you put them across makes them clearer, more readily understandable. Your presentation is merely a vehicle for your ideas. Be sure this vehicle is streamlined, up-to-date, and obviously under your control. If you go somewhere in a broken-down car, you'll get there eventually—but the trouble along the way, and the wasted time!

Carry your ideas to your listeners in a sleek, efficient vehicle that is comfortable to use and a pleasure to hear and watch. Your listeners and you, too, deserve the best.

IS SILENCE GOLDEN OR JUST YELLOW?

Silence may be golden in a hospital, in an area where students work, where intense concentration is required. Silence may mask a genius. He may never reach his potential, or he may take longer, if his thoughts are locked behind a wooden tongue.

This is the day when communication is vital, when distances between sounds can be non-existent.

In *Magic Mountain,* Thomas Mann says, "Speech is civilization itself. The word, even the most contradictory word, preserves contact—it is silence which isolates."

Join the knowledgeable ones. Broadcast your particular message, your particular opinion, with confidence and enthusiasm, with efficiency and sincerity, to better your life and help those around you. Whether you are speaking to your supervisor, your colleague, or a mass audience, let them find gold in the shape of ideas or happiness from your speech, not your silence. Withholding your opinion, your solutions, your oral support, may, indeed, not be golden—just yellow.

Public speaking begins with one speaker and one listener. Desired action may result when force takes over, but lasting action comes only when a listener is convinced mentally through communication. Influence your listener by telling him clearly and with obvious conviction.

2

Your Influence Is
Greater Than You Think

IF you're alive, you're involved with many people. Few can withdraw from the world. Why not accept the inevitable? If you have to live in the world, you must help to make it a better place. Be aware. In some cases, be apprehensive of what less enlightened people can do or are doing. Speak out—after you have thought well.

You need not be a statesman or a diplomat to shoulder the problems of the world. A war may be 10,000 miles away, but when your son or your neighbor is sent there, you are affected. Have you a way to stop the conflict? Have you read about a method to reuse water that can be adapted for your town? Universal problems have to be solved on the local level, right where you are. If you have a mind, you must use it to better your environment. If you have a voice, you must raise it to explain, to lead the way.

You are automatically part of several groups. Think about it. Who are these people who are around you, who want to listen to you or who have to listen to you?

1. Have you a family?
2. How about the people you work with?
3. What about the people in your neighborhood?
4. Do you go to church?
5. Are you a member of a club?
6. What do you do for fun?

Everywhere you go, there are people who will listen to you, people you can influence. They belong to other groups. Influence those close to you, and your ideas may travel far.

YOUR FAMILY HAS TO LISTEN

The family is perhaps the most varied collection of people and interests. Different generations, sexes, occupations, occasionally different racial cultures, religions, and political beliefs can be present.

Do you sit silently as talk flows around you, or do you discuss events of the day? Do you help with homework? Can you give reasons for supporting certain candidates? Will your teenagers listen as you express your opinions about drugs or reckless driving?

What you say at the dinner table, or a picnic, or while working in the garage may be so important that it will be repeated (not always with your name attached) to others far removed from your acquaintance. Your little voice is not so little after all.

As a teenager, my wife contested every remark her father made concerning politics and moral issues. He must have felt frustrated to meet such seeming resistance in his own home. Away from him, however, she repeated his statements. The questions he answered gave her ammunition to support her basic beliefs. She had the ear of her contemporaries. The instant and continuing bull sessions at college must have multiplied in many homes throughout the city. Even today, I hear her quote him to our sons who were born years after he was gone.

How can we possibly measure how far our spoken thoughts may travel?

YOUR CO-WORKERS HAVE EARS AND MINDS

Few of us work in an ivory tower. The people who work beside us, who meet us daily, are as involved with their surroundings as we are. They need to know how to overcome problems. Do you voice your opinion on anything beyond the weather? What is your reputation among your co-workers? Tell them what you think, but not as unsought advice! There's a way to give advice without being overbearing. You can be of inestimable help, sometimes unheralded, but you will realize a satisfaction that is its own reward.

We are all citizens as well as workers. We are all part of the activities around us. It may be a local problem that unites us: a need for a bigger hospital. It may be a national problem: a need to control the rising construction costs. It may be a world problem: contamination of the fish in the ocean.

Your future depends upon choices made by people you don't even know. But you can influence the choices of the people who you meet every day. And, in turn, their choices will affect those who represent them. The ladder to the top level is planted right where you stand. Take the first step by communicating.

COMPANIES SPREAD THEIR INFLUENCE
THROUGH THEIR SPOKESMEN

Few companies are completely self-contained or independent. They need men who can represent them at other branches, present products at conventions, describe processes at sales meetings. Knowing your particular end of the business is not enough if you want to be part of this group. You must learn to speak well, for their benefit as well as yours.

When I began working for my aerospace firm, I was thoroughly engrossed in technical developments and spent much of my spare time going to school to broaden my scientific training. As an engineer or mathematician, I wasn't expected to write very well or talk in front of an audience (I thought!).

That was fine for a beginning. As I progressed, however, and had to deal with more men, some from government agencies, others from friendly competitors, as well as foreign representatives, I discovered that facility in speaking was as necessary as technical knowledge.

Eventually, I was chosen to visit out-of-town labs and vendors with whom we were working. There is nothing more stimulating than being able to see personally the advances within your field and help others make these advances by giving them the benefit of your own experiences.

I decided I would like to attend professional conventions. What better way than to make a contribution of some sort? My opportunity arrived when a number of technical societies and government agencies called for papers. I submitted abstracts to four national organizations, hoping that one would be accepted. All four were!

Fortunately, I had enough material to enable me to present a slightly different paper to meet the specific interests of each group. After that, I was invited to lecture at many other meetings throughout the country, and a number of technical journals requested articles.

Is this type of activity solely for your own advancement? Not at all! A company is judged by the men who represent it. Develop your own ability and incidentally, your own reputation, and your company will profit as well. For, after all, what is a company but a group of men who are producing a product or a service? Their reputation rests on you.

Their influence depends upon your skill in speaking and your willingness to speak for them.

COMMUNITIES ON THE MOVE LOOK FOR LEADERSHIP

No matter how much we would like to forget our neighbors and neighborhoods and delve into some special sport or study, intelligent citizens realize they cannot escape their involvement.

If the school needs more money, a tax override has to be passed. If the hospital needs more beds, the voters must vote for a bond issue. When the YMCA needs a swimming pool for the youngsters in the less affluent section of town, someone has to excite the interest of local businessmen to raise the money. In my favorite sport, bicycle riding, we have to convince the highway designers of the need for bicycle paths.

Are you willing to wait for someone else to speak up? Why should you? If you are more than a vegetable, your community matters to you. Unless you add your voice, even on a one-to-one basis, you are not helping to make decisions for progress. And not helping to decide is making a negative decision.

Clair Burgener was a Realtor when San Diego began to expand after World War II. He became acquainted with problems that were not obvious to many engaged in minding their own small affairs, earning a living. When he had several offices throughout the city, he began to devote himself to researching and then to speaking, on community issues. Intelligent and far-seeing, he decided he could do more good in a political office.

Always well-liked within his own small circle, he has since gained a statewide reputation and has been instrumental in proposing and furthering many progressive measures. His influence is certainly effective.

Your goal may not be political, but you can enter the arena of politics to support men like Clair who have time or the type of business that permits them to serve your interests.

Will your community be better off with a new auditorium? Do minority groups need a dynamic voice from a majority sympathizer? Herb Bickley, an engineer with Toastmaster's training, regularly speaks for his community when projects affecting it come before the City Council.

Open your eyes to the surges and pressures around you. Do they need your support? Do you care enough to help? Lethargy has most of us in its grip. We flock to the outspoken vital leader. And you can be that one!

CHURCH WORK IS A CHALLENGE

Churches are always in need of leaders among their laymen. And you have a choice, neatly categorized, waiting for you. Are you the kind who prefers confrontation on an adult level? Can you identify with young people? Or do children stimulate you?

Start with the easiest group if you are fearful—teaching smaller children in Sunday School. Every faith has workbooks with broad principles laid out, specific sections of the Bible, or their own special teachings that are to be studied. You have the advantage of prepared material plus suggestions on how best to present it. But it is not all cut and dried. The questions posed will keep you awake and make you practice extemporaneous speaking. Holding a child's attention is frequently more difficult than holding the attention of a polite adult. And while a child may be critical, he is forgiving. You can make mistakes and learn from them.

Your peers, those your age, will welcome you. Join the group. See what their procedure is. When you are familiar with the needs, offer to take over for a session or two. Some of these groups follow outlines given by central boards. Others try to relate their religious ideals to events of the day. The group has the same basic beliefs as you. You can be comfortable, knowing you are among friends and that you will not be challenged on fundamentals. The principles of public speaking are the same.

Youth groups are always looking for leaders. Would you enjoy this service? Young people will listen to outsiders long before they accept the same truths openly from their parents. Apply the principles of public speaking to short talks for them. They will question your fuzzy statements. You will be needled into preparing significant reasons for any of your theories. They will be the most challenging group of all, but if you can be successful with them, you will be giving a most lasting and vital service to your community. Your ideas will be long remembered and perhaps effective for many more years.

And then there are the governing boards of every organization. Membership on these is frequently accepted as evidence of leadership by potential employers and professional organizations. Why not? Although the group is small, the techniques are the same. Effective leadership is enhanced by knowing the rules for clear communication. Leadership in a small group is the first step to leadership on a higher level.

When I first became active as a Toastmaster, I accepted a billet on one of the governing boards of my church. Later, I became chairman of that board and eventually, lay leader of the entire church. As a church ordinarily includes people from every walk of life, there were many chances to present varied programs that had to meet with approval from all these different elements.

I presided over discussions with small committees. I was master of ceremonies at a luau where more than 1,000 attended, and some of the city's top officials and celebrities were guests. The opportunities were endless.

Commander David Corey of the U.S. Coast Guard, also a Toastmaster, found his talks were so much in demand by the different churches around Portsmouth, Virginia, where he makes his home, that he has become a lay preacher and frequently substitutes for absent clergymen. With his motto "Leave it better than you found it," he has built up a well-deserved reputation in his community.

You will find more churches today want to be in the

35

forefront, if not helping to make our communities more humanitarian, at least hoping to inspire each member to live up to his often-unsuspected potential. Can you help?

Yes, you can.

1. Build up your own skills.
2. Discover what is going on in your own world.
3. Translate your understanding of the needs and fulfillments to your own congregation.

You will be invited elsewhere. Churches have their own grapevine communication. You can influence more people than you can imagine. And what's so great about it all is that you personally will grow!

THE WIDE, WIDE WORLD IS WAITING FOR YOU

You were born to be a vital part of your world. Where you exert that vitality is your decision. Discover the areas that interest you: hobbies, public service, self-help groups. Pursue the knowledge that opens the doors to a greater understanding of those skills or issues. Become an expert, but not a silent one.

Join organizations of like-minded individuals, for in unity there is strength, strength to better conditions for a hobby, a community, or a candidate. Speak out when you have an idea. Refrain from interrupting when you have nothing to add. (This is often harder!) Be available when work is to be done. Eventually, you will know so much, you will be asked to lead others, to speak to small groups of people you already know, who will hold no fears for you.

Almost every organization is allied to a similar group in another area. When you are more self-assured, you can visit them. And so it stretches till the point of international relationships is reached.

You cannot perhaps stimulate a water-skiing group to promote a political candidate, unless he has come forward with a proposition to improve local waterways. You will, on the other hand, have a strong backing when you approach the city council with a request to set aside a special area for your own skiing.

If you collect buttons, or stamps, or dolls, or bottles, or comic books, there are others who want to know about your experiences. If you like to ride a motorcycle, sail a boat, specialize in barbecue cookery, paint watercolors, weave, or drive antique autos, you can find a club. Check the lists at your Chamber of Commerce. Any group will welcome you. They're anxious to trade skills. They won't check on your grammar, but they will provide a sounding board for you to test your speaking abilities. And if you learn enough to be able to speak for them, you will be doubly welcomed.

Sitting back, watching other people perform, is an easy way to vegetate. But people who do that don't live longer. It just seems that way.

Service clubs, such as the Lions, Rotarians, Kiwanis, Optimists, are filled with men who are creative, intelligent, public-spirited, and generally, full of fun. Communities would be lost without them. They support every worthwhile drive and initiate many themselves. They need communicators.

We are not suggesting you be a joiner. Or at least, do not join too many organizations. As in everything else, strength comes from concentration. One man cannot be a good leader in too many places at once.

If you don't know where to start, try a Toastmaster or Toastmistress club. You can learn the principles, and practice weekly, receiving careful evaluations from people just like you, aware of their inadequacies in public speaking and anxious to improve themselves and help other members.

You *are* involved with life. Accept the involvement to build a better life for everyone, and you will automatically influence others who are looking for leadership. Support your interests with something more valuable than money—yourself!

3

With Understanding, You Can Influence Anyone

BEFORE you can influence anyone, you have to be sure he's listening. Who's listening to you? Not all the people who are hearing you are listening. There's a vast difference between listening and hearing. Hearing is the physical act of receiving sound waves in your ears. Listening is the process of becoming aware of the sounds and translating them into meaning. You can hear without understanding or retaining the ideas expressed.

But there are always people who *are* listening, people who you know and others of whom you are not even aware. Make your words so vital that no one will want to miss them, even though your listeners are few in number.

The size of the group, obviously, does not determine the

number of listeners. Look around in any audience. How many are keeping up with the speaker? How many are "poker faced," far away in their thoughts? The words just wash over them. Watch your own listeners. You know if you are getting through.

If your listener is accepting, agreeing, you will expand under his warmth. If he is critical, you either become heated in supporting your argument or disgusted and dry up. Listeners vary in their concentration. Look at them:

1. One person at a time—you can be almost sure to get attention.
2. People who agree with you are eager to listen.
3. Some people are uncertain. They'll listen for awhile.
4. Weary listeners are apt to drift. If you take too long, are at the end of a program, or are late in the day, your speech must be more effective.
5. Some people don't really care to listen. They're out to be seen or waste a little time. They absorb like a sponge, but they need a squeeze to react.
6. Dissenters will listen if only to object. These people have to be wooed long enough to let you speak.

People who have no pre-conceived notions or beliefs are seldom seen. But when you are presenting factual information or introducing work routines, you will find this audience.

ONE MAN LEADS TO MANY

Audiences of one are the best beginning. That, too, is public speaking. Frank Laubach gained a worldwide reputation by stressing that teaching one person at a time will reach an unlimited number. His program was devoted to teaching reading and language skills to the illiterate. He found that students carrying his teachings, one by one, pyramided his voice and lessons. Why not apply this principle yourself?

Do you have difficulty in holding one person's attention? Analyze the reasons. We all know people who have magnetic personalities. Whenever they appear, others turn to them, eager to absorb their words. Sometimes we listen because we know what they say is worthwhile; sometimes we listen because they tell a good story.

Next time you are at a picnic, or a cocktail party, or any gathering, observe them. Listen not only to their words but also watch their attitude. They do not grab lapels and physically force people to listen to them. Maybe they "grab" with their eyes. In all likelihood, the grabbing they do is largely with their words and ideas. But as in everything else, the whole person is important. Their subjects excite them. They communicate their mood and infect others with this mood.

When you have reached the point where you can transmit your enthusiasm to others with no conscious effort, you have arrived. Whether your audience numbers one or 100 is immaterial. You are communicating. You are thereby influencing or informing or entertaining.

Since you've got to begin somewhere, begin with that one man or woman beside you.

EACH MAN STANDS AT THE CENTER OF THE UNIVERSE

The universe revolves around your listener. Or at least, it feels that way to him. How can you persuade him to do something? You must look at your request or subject from his viewpoint. Why should he come to a club picnic, attend your church, or consider your candidate for office?

Millard Bennett, a public speaker, tells the story of one of his experiments. One evening, he was reading a newspaper in his living room, his wife seated nearby.

He was very tired, but he was also thirsty. He knew his wife would get him a glass of water if he asked, but he thought, "I make my living by persuading others to do what I suggest. Let's see if I can make her get me that water without being obvious about it."

He opened his campaign by remembering a particularly fine dinner they had shared in which a succulent

Smithfield ham was featured. His descriptions were so vivid that in no time at all, his wife was thirsty. When she went to get herself some water, he "discovered" he was thirsty, too, and would appreciate a drink. It took a bit longer, but he was applying the principles of persuasion that we could all use on one or many listeners.

The relationship between two levels of employees is always influenced by the smoothness of their communication. Certainly, no man can advance in his profession if he cannot explain his ideas or influence those who work for him, or over him, to proceed along more desirable lines.

Are you afraid to approach your superior? You may have a perfect right to be. He may have erected seemingly impenetrable barriers, but generally, a little subtlety will work wonders.

Tell him, "I don't like the way that light is placed. The glare bothers my eyes." If he's compassionate, and there's available money, he may do something about it.

You can say, "Don't you think that placing the light over in that corner would cut down the glare and make the processing more accurate and possibly quicker?"

He may say "no," but to what is he saying "no?". His viewpoint is focussed on the production process, not on you. And it is his responsibility to produce the best possible work in the least possible time.

You may manage to manipulate his thinking so that he feels moving the light is his own idea.

Say, "I know or feel I could do the work quicker if my eyes didn't tire from the glare."

Persuading those who work for you is as important as persuading those who supervise you. And, as always, concentrate on your listeners, not on yourself. Lead them to an idea, and be delighted when they discover it for themselves.

You know the improvement or suggestion will benefit you or support your program. They may realize this, too, but it is secondary. If you really want action, make it worth your listener's while, physically, mentally, or spiritually, and you will know success.

LEVEL WITH YOUR LISTENER

Would you explain the purposes of a desalinization plant in the same words to engineers as you would to a junior high school class? Would you discuss shutter speeds in the same detail with amateur photographers as you would with professionals?

As the speaker, persuader, or informer, you have the responsibility of determining where your listener is, from the point of understanding, ability, or background, because that's where you must begin.

This does not mean "talking down" to the less-informed. Very young children are as aware as adults of this attitude, and all resent it. Technical words may be beyond their educational level, but most broad principles can be understood by everyone. A five-syllable word that combines a number of meanings may be a shortcut, but not if you lose your listener. Use more words, simpler words. Use pictures, diagrams. Err on the side of simplicity rather than expect too much comprehension.

Don't waste time on impossibilities. Accept the fact that for reasons of environment, heredity, or economics, some people just cannot be persuaded. The reasons may be physical or emotional, but they must be acknowledged.

SOME LISTENERS ALREADY AGREE WITH YOU

Most people who listen to you will be agreeable. As you progress in public speaking, you will find this is particularly true of larger groups. After all, they have taken the trouble to come, to listen, and hopefully, to understand.

Unfortunately, this sort of response often encourages

laziness. Don't fall into this trap. Exert yourself to underline their beliefs with interesting sidelights and comments. Enlarge their knowledge. Put life into your theme with touches of humor or anecdotes or personal experiences.

They believe in you, now. There may be a day when you have to persuade them against their own ideas. Build your reputation, whether your listener is one man or more. Pave the way to future acceptance.

SOME LISTENERS ARE WILLING TO BE CONVINCED

The Mugwumps—those with their mugs on one side of the fence and their wumps on the other—can be found in almost every audience, not just in politics. They can see good on both sides. They want to be informed. They want to do the right thing.

Marshal your arguments carefully. Do your research well, finding all the information that is available. If you have established your reputation in a previous meeting, you are well ahead; otherwise, you must justify your authority to make a wise decision and solicit support. Convince your listener of your genuineness.

No matter how many people are listening, the principles are the same. Remember, if you convince one man, he may convince others.

SOME LISTENERS ARE TOO TIRED TO CARE

So what have you got to say that's more interesting than reading the newspaper—or, if you're a PTA leader, more interesting than watching a comedy special on television?

A humble approach won't help matters. Your opening sentence must carry plenty of punch. Startle your listener.

If you're on a platform, move around. Eye movement keeps him awake until you can make another challenging remark.

Change your voice pitch. Tell a joke or two if you can find an appropriate one. Be primed with anecdotes to illustrate your points.

You will have to work harder, physically as well as mentally. Still, you are constantly building your reputation as a man worth listening to. If you want action, and you care enough to make the effort to stimulate this group, make it worth your while by putting in that extra punch.

Keep your listener awake and absorbed. You may be lucky enough to have him act—or, at the very least, want to listen, next time you have something to say.

SOME LISTENERS BRING THE BODY
BUT TURN OFF THE EARS

The smug, the aloof, are occasionally corralled into coming to a meeting. They've been everywhere; they've heard everything. Who are you to tell them what to do?

They are the most difficult group to stimulate, for they have erected a sound barrier against you. They are frustrating and tend to undermine your self-confidence. Avoid any confrontation with them until you are certain of yourself. And then, speak out with a surge of confidence. Remember, if you belittle yourself, they will accept an even lower estimate of your abilities and background.

As in a good fight, refuse to accept any idea of defeat. Go in with a good defense. Shock them! Make a seemingly impossible statement that you can back up with facts. Use brutal, but not offensive, language.

A local minister resorts to these tactics. Most of his congregation agree that they are frequently startled. Many feel he is not so godly as his counterpart across town, but he is easier to listen to. And he is preaching the same ideas.

"God damn it to hell!" Henry Ward Beecher shouted to his congregation one Sunday. You can picture the stunned silence that followed. "That's what I heard a man say yesterday," he continued, "My sermon this morning is going to be on blasphemy."

You believe in your ideas. Make your audience listen, and they, too, may believe.

SOME LISTENERS HAVE CHIPS ON THEIR SHOULDERS

We all mingle with people who thoroughly disagree with us in one or another segment of our thinking. We may attend the same church or work together but support different political parties. Open your mouth to speak about your opposing ideas, and this listener closes his mind. He is either blind with rage at your stupidity, or he is mentally rounding up his brilliant opposition.

A frontal attack merely arouses a quick defense. You've got to ambush him, sneak up on him. Introduce a topic on which you can agree. With individuals, you can be selective. Before a larger group, you have to fall back on the accepted conventions. Politicians do this by speaking of motherhood, the flag, or "good old" American apple pie.

Go from the agreeable topic to still another agreeable idea. Your listener relaxes. You're not such a bad guy after all. You do support the right things. He's willing to listen a little longer.

At this point, you can hint, but very gently, about your hostile idea. If he shows signs of defiance or flight, try another accepted topic. Eventually, you will have to get to the subject, but you have warmed up your listener, and if you can discover in this preliminary skirmish the right psychological approach, you have a better chance of persuading him, or at least making him wonder if he is so completely right in his own thoughts.

Handling more than one opponent at a time merely multiplies the problem. Practice convincing one man against his pre-conceived idea. You will have to use the same technique on a larger scale with more people when you feel easier and more skillful.

If you know your listener disagrees with you, it is even more important to look at the problem from his viewpoint. Would you waste time convincing a one-legged man that jogging is fun? The town's leading Republican will never openly support any Democratic candidate.

If, in the course of your efforts, you discover your listener is becoming more belligerent, back off. His emotions have been aroused, and his reason is smothered. Retreat to "fight" another day.

Persuading anyone to support a new idea or course of action is satisfying; persuading a man who is opposed to your ideas is even more satisfying.

THIS ABOVE ALL

Where the occasion permits, remember that humor is a great leveler. Everyone enjoys a laugh.

Keep your jokes clean, clear, and relevant. If you can't tell a joke properly, study the chapter on humor. Whether or not you ever stand upon a platform, this technique is valuable and can be learned.

Picture yourself in front of an audience. Picture them intent and interested. Realize now that you can stimulate anyone: the critical, the bored, the hostile. You are capable of anything you choose to do. The first step is the desire, and by reading this book and following its suggestions, you are building the frame to support this picture.

Section II

YOUR SUBJECT

4

Influence Rests
Upon Knowledge

WHAT excites or annoys you? Most of us put up with all sorts of discomforts out of sheer inertia. But there comes a time when an oversensitive spot is touched. Then, we react. Can we react meaningfully?

Before you speak with a desire to sway others, ask yourself these questions:

1. Do I feel strongly about this issue?
2. Do I know enough?
3. Can I talk to anyone who knows more than I do?
4. How much information should I include?

If you answer "yes" to the first question, you can take care of the others.

If you have strong opinions, you are the best qualified to speak for them. No one can represent your ideas as well as you. Many customs or traditions disappear, and many praiseworthy projects fail, not because they are not wanted or appreciated, but because no one cared enough to take positive action.

WHY TRY TO INFLUENCE ANYONE?

With so many millions of people inhabiting our own country, a lot of details can be overlooked—details that build up to huge menaces before they are caught and corrected. The average citizen is forced to spend most of his thinking time earning a living. He needs watchdogs to alert him.

Luckily, a few aware members of society concern themselves with community problems. One-sentence news items in the local papers often point the way to a potential hazardous development. That's where you come in. Sound the alarm.

One young girl was so concerned about the imprisonment of the *USS Pueblo* crew by the North Koreans that she began a special prayer program that expanded from the attention of her schoolmates to the whole city. Despite the fact that she was only 15 at the time, she influenced a great many people. Her crusade may not have affected the actual liberation of the men, but who knows? Great programs start with one man or woman.

During the student riots, young leaders came to the fore. Chris Barr, a Harvard student, at home in California for the summer, offered to speak to any group about the various student movements. A number of local clubs were interested, and Chris spent his summer off-hours in bridging the generation gap we hear so much about. Chris, as a high school student, had developed his speaking skills and won a number of prizes throughout the community.

You have the same opportunity. People really want to know why. They would like to support a sensible project. They would like to raise their voices against injustice or haphazard planning. But they won't spend their time discovering what is going on. Tell them. Tell them what to do about it.

Maybe you are not so involved in public projects. Maybe you just want to share your enthusiasm for a trip you've taken. Or perhaps you managed to grow an exotic plant that you haven't seen anywhere else in your area. Garden club members will be delighted to listen to your story.

Ray Sodomka, professionally a tool engineer, but an ardent leisure-time gardener, gave a talk one evening on how to use plastic throw-away materials in the garden. His ideas were ingenious. Today, years after that ten-minute talk, we use many of his suggestions.

Another evening, an aerospace administrator, Joseph Skibinski, talked for about eight minutes on how to clean a paintbrush. Skibinski is a careful man who believes in using the best equipment, but he knows that most people abuse theirs. Like Sodomka's information, the techniques we learned in that short talk have been very useful.

If you are an ardent hobbyist, tell people what you are doing. Let them enjoy your enthusiasms, too. Senior citizens and adolescents are looking for attractive hobbies to fill their leisure hours.

You may not add to your income by sharing your experiences, but you will gain a feeling of well-being in the knowledge that you have given others a chance to grow. And you never can tell when some listener may remember you when something worthwhile does come along. We call this old policy, "casting bread upon the waters." And it's not to be scorned!

BE SURE YOU KNOW ENOUGH

If you are going to offer yourself as a serious speaker, you will need more material at your fingertips than you plan to present. Do you know the available material? Perhaps you'd better refresh your knowledge.

Start with encyclopedias. You may have overlooked interesting or vital ramifications of your subject. General encyclopedias are not always interchangeable. Some concentrate on lengthy, broad treatments; others use short, factual paragraphs. The best encyclopedias are:

- *Encyclopedia Britannica*-Long scholarly articles; revised constantly. An American publication despite its title. Be sure to use volume 24 to locate the exact information.
- *Encyclopedia Americana*-Fairly long articles; particularly strong on American towns and cities.
- *World Book*-Highly recommended; lucid explanations; short articles with many illustrations and cross-references.

There are a few special encyclopedias in every field. Just to mention a few:

- *Grove's Dictionary of Music and Musicians.* Nine volumes and a supplement.
- *McGraw-Hill Encyclopedia of Science and Technology.* 15 volumes.
- Hartnell, Phyllis, editor. *Oxford Companion to the Theatre.*
- Pratt, John. *The Official Encyclopedia of Sports.*

STATISTICS ARE GREAT TO BACK UP A STATEMENT

Many people consider statistics dull. Others say that statistics can prove any point. In any event, they add greatly to a talk, if not quoted interminably. Be sure the figures are significant. Many books can be used to discover the facts.

Almost everyone knows the *World Almanac,* perhaps the most useful and comprehensive collection of miscellaneous information. Two others to be found in every public library are:

- U.S. Bureau of the Census. *Statistical Abstract*-Published annually, with figures going back 15 or 20 years. Some go as far back as 1789.
- *Statesman's Yearbook*-Published annually since 1864; a statistical and historical survey of the states of the world, with emphasis on the United States and the United Kingdom.

There are handbooks for every country and statistical compilations on many subjects which will add color to any talk.

PUT PEOPLE IN THE PICTURE

Do you know the biographical dictionaries? Most subjects have a "name" connected with them.

- *Who's Who* and *Who's Who in America*-Brief factual information about important living people.
- *Current Biography*-First published in 1940; comes out annually in bound volumes with monthly paper supplements. A cumulative index can be found in the latest bound volume. Living celebrities in every field and from everywhere are described in long articles, always accompanied by a picture and a bibliography.
- *Webster's Biographical Dictionary*-Useful for a brief identification and correct pronunciation.
- *Dictionary of American Biography* and the *Dictionary of National Biography*-Many-volumed sets; published early in this century. Excellent to identify people who were not famous enough to be included in encyclopedias.

As in encyclopedias, there are special biographical dictionaries for almost every profession and country.

USE BOOKS TO EXPAND YOUR BASIC IDEAS

Card catalogs are indexes to books available in the library. If you have not learned how to use one, don't hesitate to ask your librarian to explain. For various reasons, mostly financial, libraries use shortcuts, so card catalogs are not always the same. They are, however, all easily understood.

If your library hasn't enough material, you can find the names of books available elsewhere. Specialized bibliographies in book form can be found, or you may use the *Publishers' Trade List Annual.* If the library does not have one, most booksellers will be glad to let you look through their copies.

This annual set comes out in specialized volumes: author, title, subject, and publisher. This lists only the books *currently* being printed.

MAGAZINES-PAMPHLETS-PAPERS BRING YOU UP-TO-DATE

Perhaps all you want to do is bring your material up-to-date. For that, you will need periodical indexes.

- *Reader's Guide to Periodical Literature*-Indexes more than 150 magazines over a wide range of subjects:

  Business Week, Good Housekeeping, Mechanics Illustrated, Christian Century, Catholic World, Yachting, Popular Photography, Ebony, and so on. The material is arranged under subjects with many cross-references. How to use the indexed information is explained in each volume.

Like encyclopedias and yearbooks, there are specialized indexes to the more specialized periodicals.

- *Social Sciences and Humanities Index*-Covers about 175 scholarly American and English periodicals.
- *Public Affairs Information Service*-Also includes books, documents, and pamphlets.
- *Art Index.*
- *Education Index.*

There are others in other fields, although you must be aware that the more technical you get, the less likely you will be able to find the materials in smaller libraries.

Most libraries have their own vertical files full of material they think may be of value to their readers. If you have a special project, let your librarian know. She'll be delighted to add that subject to her file and catch any passing material for you. Your library may even subscribe to the *Vertical File Service,* a monthly listing of pamphlets, paperbacks, and other more or less ephemeral material, that is usually free or inexpensive.

One other reference book to update your subject should be of value. The *New York Times Index,* published yearly since

1913, is called the "master key." Why? Because, by furnishing you the date of a specific event, it unlocks the treasure chest of your own local papers for any national or international activity. Using the index alone may supply sufficient information for your needs.

If you're one of those lucky enough to have a large library nearby, you can chase your story down on microfilm.

INTERVIEWS ADD COLOR AND LIFE TO ANY SUBJECT

If your subject can be updated with fresh material not yet recorded, your remarks will be even more vital. Talk to people who are involved. Few people refuse to talk.

There are three things that are essential if you do interviews:

1. Be sure to make an appointment. Just barging in on a busy person is unpardonable. Even if, to all apparent views, he seems unoccupied, ask for permission to take up his time.
2. Don't go in "cold." Have specific questions ready. You may not need them, but they may be necessary to guide your interviewee's remarks so that he can supply you with the material you want. Try to use questions that cannot be answered "yes" or "no."
3. Having digested the material, let him see, in written form, approximately what you plan to say, particularly if you quote him directly. Tell him in the beginning of the interview that you plan to do this. He's more likely to tell you more if he's sure you won't misquote him.

Occasionally, a man may be willing to have his remarks tape-recorded. There are some who will refuse.

If the machine is out, notes seldom are. An old Chinese proverb says "The strongest memory is lighter than the palest ink." Don't trust your memory.

NOTE-TAKING IS AN ART IN ITSELF

Note-taking is an essential part of researching. And like

everything else, there's a right way and a wrong way. Keep your notes on cards or slips of paper. The small 3 x 5 size are the handiest, as they fit into any pocket or handbag. Skimping on the number of these cards, or paper, is an extravagant mistake.

Every fact should be noted on a separate card, with the source on the back, including the page number. If it's from an interview, include the date and location as well. If the quote is exact, put quotation marks around it. Later on, you can write subject headings above each fact for quick identification. When you are ready to assemble your information, these cards can be arranged to suit your purposes.

DON'T TELL THEM EVERYTHING

Sure, your subject is fascinating. You may have been thinking about it for a long time—maybe even 20 years.

Be selective. Choose the most vital, or amusing, or up-to-the-minute facet of your subject and build from that. You can indicate that there's a lot more to discover, that you've only touched the peaks. You can tell them how to learn more, give them sources of information so they can pursue the topic further.

What should be your focal point? You could start with the origin of your subject. But why? A discussion of our policies in the Far East does not necessarily include Commodore Perry's opening up trade centers in the nineteenth century. That the Vietnamese have been pursuing a civil war for more than 600 years is interesting, but is it important in this talk? Of course, analogies may be made, but don't be caught in a net of obscure details. Don't populate your forest with so many trees that no one can see any path clearly.

How many times do you find speakers dwelling on the fact that Joe Smith, who is running for assemblyman, has 12 children? Just what is this meant to prove? Maybe he has the interests of the future at heart because his many children will need a better world in which to live. But then again, with all those children, has he time to devote to your problems? If you must bring in seemingly irrelevant facts, tell us why.

Some people love their material so much that they go on and on till the saturation point is reached, and their audience loses all interest. Watch your audience. Be prepared to cut your talk when interest lags. There's an old adage, "It is more blessed to talk too little than too much, for speech to be immortal need not be eternal."

While watching the audience is the easiest way to determine their interest, it is more efficient to limit your thoughts to a comprehensible quantity before you start. Crispness and clarity are your goals. A vast store of information is vital to you, but don't smother your listeners with too much.

DON'T HOG THE SHOW

You know your subject thoroughly. Why bother to bring in someone else? Why introduce anecdotes illustrating other people's experiences? No matter how interesting our individual lives are to us, they just don't hold the same appeal for everyone else—unless, perhaps, you are a fabulously important celebrity. Even then, self-centered talks or personal pronouncements can be monotonous.

There are many collections of quotations that will give you an abundant selection of short, pithy remarks which can add sparkle to any talk. Here are a few that most libraries carry:

- Stevenson, Burton E. *Home Book of Quotations*-50,000 arranged by subject.
- Bartlett, John. *Familiar Quotations*-Arranged chronologically by authors, with special sections on the *Bible* and other great works.
- Simpson, James. *Contemporary Quotations*-A newer collection arranged by subject.
- Braude, Jacob M. *New Treasury of Stories for Every Speaking and Writing Occasion.*

There are many others, all excellent in their own right,

and many of them are in paperback form as well. If you are planning to speak more than once, they are valuable additions to your personal library.

ENJOY YOURSELF

Anything you enjoy doing can be done easily. If it distresses you to talk to a large group on a large subject, don't—not until you have had some experience.

If you're not sold on the issue to be discussed, don't attempt to sell it. Lukewarm support is valueless.

Begin with a small group. Begin with something that interests you—something that is so important you can't control your enthusiasm, or something that incites you to protest without hesitation. Be so well-informed that extra material wells up inside of you. No question will daunt you.

Then, forget yourself. Your subject—not you—is what catches the audience. Your goal is to bring them together. Your emotions were stimulated originally by your subject. Transmit those sensations. Appeal to your listeners' emotions. There is a charisma, an electric warmth, that develops. Enjoy your ability to help your listeners grow.

5

People Have to
Listen and Understand
to Be Influenced

YOUR research is finished. Before you begin to organize your thoughts, take time to remember the essential components of each speech. As in any good recipe, there will be one or two optional ingredients that can be omitted. But not many.

Whether the speech is long or short, to one person or 1,000, these standards must be observed. They are almost too obvious to mention. Still, a speaker who is sincere, devoted, and well-grounded, may forget them in his concentration on material alone.

What are these basics?

1. Use simple language.
2. Be relevant.
3. Be orderly.
4. Relate your subject to people.
5. If possible, have the audience participate.
6. Add a third dimension with movement, visual aids, and sound.
7. Inject humor.
8. Appeal to the emotions when possible.
9. Fit the allotted time.
10. Have a meaningful conclusion.

Keep this list handy. Check it every time you prepare a speech. Check it again when your speech is finished. Have you overlooked any points?

SIMPLICITY IS NOT SIMPLE

Keeping it simple seems the easiest thing in the world. Not really. Simplicity is relative. What is easily understandable to an aerospace engineer dealing with cryogenics is not always understandable to an engineer in automotive design. And as for the multitude, it's a completely unknown world.

Consider the more familiar. Even then, you cannot assume your audience has your background or vocabulary. For example, in a garden club, everyone should know what a conifer is. But there may be a guest. Make your remark clear: "When it comes to planting conifers, those stately cone-bearing pines ..."

At a conference, during a discussion of problems of the European Common Market, American experts were stumped every time they heard the words "inedible horticultural products." It was not until later that they discovered they were discussing flowers.

Not only should your language be clear, but also your sentences should be short. Talking is different from reading. In reading, a student can go back to analyze the remark. In speaking, if a sentence can be easily broken into two, your ideas are probably more understandable that way. Be crisp in your language so that the thoughts may emerge with clarity.

Someone remarked that there are a few times in life when we really listen, comprehend, and act. The man who comes in and yells "Fire!" has no difficulty in communicating.

Wouldn't it be great if all ideas were that easy to communicate? Since they are not, be sure that you, as a speaker, present no barriers to understanding.

IS THAT FACT NECESSARY?

Keep to your subject. Sometimes you may need to substantiate your argument with historical background, but don't divert too much time from your main theme. Discussing American involvement in Vietnam does not require delving into the history of the country. A sentence or two to add color or basis for a specific statement is helpful, but remember it is accessory to, not the basis of, your talk.

BE ORDERLY

There is seldom a right order for any presentation. Your decision about how to introduce the material is your own. You can begin at the beginning and work forward. You can begin at the end and flash back to the beginning.

You may want to start with the most important idea first, then mention lesser points. Maybe, you'd rather build to a dramatic conclusion.

If you have collected your material on individual cards, lay them out on the table like a game of solitaire. Try several arrangements until you come to the one that, in your opinion, *you* can handle with the most ease and power.

EVERYTHING IN LIFE IS CENTERED ON PEOPLE

Whether we are trying to communicate with distant stars or digging to the center of the earth, people are involved. Not only are they involved, but the results will involve other people. Most people want to hear about others. Be sure you include this kind of material.

If your company produced 50 planes last year, tell your listeners not only the statistics, but also something about the workers or the potential passengers. If one of the field engineers had a pertinent or interesting experience with a customer, tell about it.

Photographers may be intent upon technical information, but again, personalities add color. Slip in a slide of a child watching a pet turtle or a senior citizen resting in the sun.

An anecdote is more interesting if a name is tied to it, not necessarily a famous name. If no name is available, characterize the person of whom you are speaking. Don't say "an Italian." Be more specific. "An eager young Italian butcher in Rapallo" gives the man a rounded image, a personality.

Be a name-dropper, not for self-aggrandizement, but to bring life into your talk.

LET YOUR LISTENERS CONTRIBUTE

A man who is contributing to your speech is a listening man. The contribution may be no more than a smile or a nod of his head.

Throw out a related question or two when you think you are losing contact. Have your listeners raise their hands in reply.

"How many of you saw the World Series game on television?"

"How many of you voted in the last election?"

Movement alone will be welcome to your audience, who may be vitally interested in your ideas, but are tired of sitting still.

Some parsons find their important ideas accompanied with "Amen, brother." They know the congregation is listening.

Politicians call for cheers. Pep rallies inspire chanting of success slogans.

Some programs use audience members to demonstrate principles they have been discussing. Others accept questions as they go along.

Be careful, however, to keep the participation in directed channels. Never let the audience take over. If you do, you are satisfying those who participate, but others may feel they are losing because they expected to hear you and your ideas.

There are many ways you can keep the audience awake, listening, and inspired. The easiest and most successful way is to have them join you in developing your ideas.

EXTEND BEYOND YOURSELF

Props, visual or vocal, can add depth or meaning to your words.

Discuss the results of litter, and you will reach most of your audience. Show a picture of Lake Hemet, its waters crowded with beer cans, and the audience's audible response will demonstrate their understanding. Talk about how much of your tax dollar is devoted to welfare, in relation to education, and your audience may be able to keep the figures and relationships in mind. Display a large pie-shaped graph, and you will know the differences can be seen immediately.

Block diagrams are direct, easily made, easily understood.

Posters add interest. Ray Harter, a Toastmaster in San Diego, gives a whimsical talk on how to milk a whale, using a number of simple cartoons he has drawn himself. They are always greeted with shouts of laughter.

Use a chalkboard if it's helpful. Be sure to face your audience as you discuss what you've written or drawn. Be sure, too, that your audience can see it.

Sometimes, you can produce sounds. Phil Ferdig brings his wife along to sing phrases or single notes to illustrate some ideas. In one of his talks, Scott Carpenter introduced a tape recording of President Johnson's congratulations when the astronauts returned to earth. No amount of description could have produced the atmosphere and humor the audience realized from that.

Bring along a sample or a product. Ben McCart conducts experiments with Amway products and its rivals when he is trying to influence his listeners to buy from him.

Moving around on the platform is the simplest way to attract attention while you are speaking. If your talk does not lend itself to external visual or aural stimulation, remember that the audience is watching you, that you have a repertory of movements available, from raising your eyebrows to jumping.

To influence anyone, you have to catch his attention. Do that by every means at your disposal, as well as talking.

EVERYONE ENJOYS A LAUGH

When whimsy or wit is included, your speech will hold your audience.

Choose your quips or jokes for their relevance. Weave them into your talk so they are part of the whole pattern.

Be sure they are acceptable to everyone, and try to use fresh material. If you have old material, perhaps you can give it an up-to-date twist. Remember, however, that some old jokes are like good music. They can be enjoyed again and again.

Let that subconscious of yours go to work. Over a number of days, you will discover material rising to your consciousness from your memory banks. Relevant stories will catch your eye as you read.

A touch of humor is like a sudden ray of sunlight in a storm, enjoyed by everyone.

EMOTIONS MOVE PEOPLE TO ACTION

Recognize the strong emotions in man. Love, hate, fear are the top three. Can you arouse these in your listener?

In college, our football coach, during the half-time, consciously made us furious with our opponents. We performed with greater zeal after each pep talk.

Love is a more lasting emotion—stronger, too. Politicians who appeal to our love of our country, of our locality, of our family, are successful when they personalize the emotion.

Fear, unfortunately, is negative, but a way of life for many, and should be recognized. Many people do the right thing because they're afraid to do otherwise.

There are lesser emotions—disgust, grief, joy, sympathy, envy—that can be used.

Any subject can be a dry recital of facts or formulas. Relate these facts to your audience so that their emotions are stirred.

If you are appalled at the number of superhighways being constructed, go beyond the statistics. Describe the losses of wildlife and scenic areas, appealing to your listener's love for his country. Arouse his hatred at the air pollution he will be subject to as a result of more cars, his grief at the invasion of his recreational areas by outsiders.

Can you think of any subject that has no emotional possibilities? Check your talk to be sure you have stirred your listener.

BE A CLOCK-WATCHER

Consider your timing. You may be thoroughly engrossed in your subject, willing to give all your facts, all your strength. Not so your audience. There will be a few as interested as you, but save your second line of revelations for them alone at another time or after the talk.

Everyone lives by a schedule. If you are allotted ten minutes, fit your talk to meet that time slot. In Toastmaster Clubs, speakers are penalized for missing their timing by more than 15 seconds in either direction.

Speeches can be short: "He came. He saw. He conquered." Speeches may be long. Edmund Burke in his famous speech on "Conciliation with America," had only two points, yet he took more than two hours to deliver this dynamic 20,000-word address. Whatever time you are given, accept it. Before you appear, arrange your material to fit.

YOUR CONCLUSION MUST BE STRONG

Your speech is pointed to your conclusion. Be sure your listeners are told plainly and clearly the reason they are listening, as your last remark:

"Go out and vote for Gerry Thomas."

"Send your contribution to Project Concern."

"Keep those poisons away from your children."

Sure, you've been telling your audience the same thing in one form or another all through your talk. But leave no doubt about it as you finish. A short, positive statement is clear, strong, and motivating.

WHAT IT ALL ADDS UP TO

You can only influence people who listen to you. Observe these ten basic principles and you will have your audience awake, aware, and understanding.

6

Decide on the Best Way to Influence Your Listener

MOST talks have built-in formats. Decide why you are talking.

1. Are you telling a novice how to do something?
2. Are you relating an experience or an adventure?
3. Are you persuading a group to support a drive or a candidate, or to change from an old way of doing or thinking?
4. Are you out to inspire people, give them understanding or self-confidence?
5. Do you want to make your listeners laugh and enjoy the present?

You have a many-faceted personality. Your interests

spread in diverse directions. You have plenty of reasons to talk. Under some circumstances, you have a responsibility to talk. You may not be a platform speaker right now. But you do have the essentials: a subject and specialized knowledge or ideas on the subject. You can, indeed, influence your listener to follow certain techniques or question his past beliefs.

FOR INFORMATION ONLY

Most of us have spent our lives learning by listening. From the cradle, our parents tell us what to do or how to do everything. A questioning young daughter sent one father to the encyclopedia to overcome his ignorance about the stars. All the elements of an informational talk to a group were called into use.

Practice on your children. When they ask questions, seize the opportunity to learn as well as communicate. Children are adept at wiggling away if your technique is poor. Teenagers are particularly difficult to hold. If you succeed with them, by verbal communication alone, you can succeed with almost anyone.

An informative talk is the most common of all speeches. Less sophisticated speaking ability is required. Most of the people you are addressing need no motivation. They listen because they need to know or want to learn.

Let us assume you have been asked to talk on a specific subject you are expected to know, at work or to a group who share the same interest with you. Presumably, you need not dig into volumes for facts and figures. Still, you should have about three times as much material in your mind as you expect to introduce. You might, in fact, find ramifications you have not considered before, if you do spend some time looking into the subject with an open mind.

Before you start, write down three things:

1. My purpose in this talk.
2. The points I must cover.
3. How can my listeners use this information?

Decide upon the answers early. Look at the list from time to time. Let the points you have outlined simmer in your subconscious. This last you do without trying, but be aware that the process is going on. You will discover anecdotes, interesting side facts, perhaps related humor will drift to the surface of your mind. Jot down these ideas. There is nothing so fleeting as an uncaptured thought.

Begin with a definite statement of your purpose. Throughout your talk, go back and refer to this statement. Not only will it be helpful for your listeners, but also it will keep you from rambling.

Your purpose is to impart information that is necessary or important. Be ready to expand in a questioning period if necessary, but to be sure your audience is retaining the vital facts, concentrate on them. You will, of course, have to know your audience and prepare your material to suit them.

Too much information may confound your listeners. If the subject is new to them, they may have no way of determining the relative importance of your facts. Unfortunately, a willing mind can absorb only so much. If you want to put forth a wealth of information for the more advanced, point out as you go along what is beyond basic material.

Be selective, but not repetitive. Produce charts and pictures. Show enthusiasm in your voice, your movements, your choice of words. You are sharing with them something that you have enjoyed or understood. Influence comes in this talk when you convince your listeners that there is a right way to do things, or there is pleasure to be found in a new understanding or skill.

SHARE YOUR EXPERIENCES

When conversation proceeds beyond the basic needs, man likes to share his experiences. Vicarious adventures are enjoyable if the narrator has a desire to inform or entertain.

There's a constant demand for travelers to show their

slides and artifacts from less-traveled places. You don't have to sell any thing or any place. These talks have all the elements of most platform speeches and can be practiced on your friends, without their being aware of their guinea pig status.

You may have taken a safari through Kenya, muled down into the Grand Canyon, trudged around the Tower of London, or spent an afternoon watching the Polish dancers in the park. So long as you are enthusiastic about your subject, you can find an audience.

Besides having an interesting subject, however, you must know the facts. Nothing is more disconcerting than to have one of your viewers correct a statement. If you aren't sure, say so.

Try to have a unique approach. One artist took her fellow artists on a pictorial trip around Europe. She had visited most of the tourist spots in her year abroad, but her pictures were not views of the much-touted buildings and statues. She showed a back canal in Venice, taken in the fall, then again in the spring. A huge oak with the sun coming in at an angle could have been anywhere. This is Normandy, she declared. Children eating delicacies or conventional food from their own countries were frequent subjects. She included many shots of scarred, crumbling homes, their faults masked by gay petunias and geraniums. They were not very different from many local abandoned farmhouses, but the angle was special and personal.

The talk had universal interest. She was enthusiastic. She had been selective. And most of all, she had accompanied almost every picture with an anecdote related to people.

Perhaps you think your artifacts or slides will carry any performance—they won't! Your stories or your side comments are as important as the objects on display.

Selectivity is vital. One of the local prize-winning photographers took a series of pictures on a recent trip to Yucatan. There, he visited the well-known shrine of Chichén Itzá. He was so enthusiastic about the place, that many outsiders who heard him say he was going to show his slides at a meeting asked to attend.

Modestly, he admitted he had taken about 3,500 views. That should have warned us. He showed 200. And every one was of the temple. Some looked up to the highest point. Some looked down from the highest point. We saw the central steps from one angle—at daybreak, at noon, at sunset. We understood why he showed a series of the same view when different filters were used. After all, the show was for a camera club. But even the most ardent devotee must have secretly rested his eyes in weariness.

People can take just so much. Even when they are delighted with a talk, we must remember that the mind can absorb only what the seat can endure. Leave your audience wanting more. They will come back if they feel you have something to offer. Be aware. Be sensitive to the rustling, the coughing, the side-whispering. If you're sure your subject isn't boring in itself, maybe you are on too long.

Anecdotes and short stories hold attention. Reach out and make up something if necessary. Preface it with, "I've always wondered what would have happened that day if . . ." Manufactured stories are acceptable if they contain elements of possibility and are used to illustrate a point.

An enterprising deputy sheriff in a small town in Colorado is a natural story-teller. He has little or no opportunity to use this talent in the ordinary course of events, but he found an outlet.

Perched on a ledge at the entrance to the San Juan Mountains, Ouray, Colorado, is a typical roadside town with small business interests, a remnant of the days when silver mining was thriving. The motel owner, where we checked in for the night, told us there would be a slide show for anyone who cared to watch, that evening, in the community hall down the street. Ordinarily, most of the audience would never have contemplated attending, but there they were, literally a captive audience. Some, of course, bedded down without thought of going. But the others were glad to do something.

Marvin Gregory, our host, told us who he was and that

he thought we were privileged to visit this most unusual spot. Well, it was beautiful, we all agreed. But no more so than any other town in this most spectacular of states. We settled down, expecting nothing much.

But we had reckoned without the imagination and showmanship of this wiry Coloradan. Admittedly, he had been doing this for years. He had learned the technique of pleasing as well as educating the audience.

When the lights came up at the end, most of the tourists were enthusiastic, making plans to stay longer. They didn't want to miss the jeep trips up the mountain to see the abandoned mines, the flowers that grew only at high altitudes, any of a number of things he had described or illustrated with his pictures. A story or two accompanied each subject. He had tales for every type of listener.

He was so enthusiastic about his town that he could not keep it to himself. He presented something that meant so much to him that he ended up influencing everyone who heard him.

HOW TO STIMULATE ACTION

Many talks carry with them the desire of the speaker to persuade his audience to a new belief or, more important, to some form of action. Most speakers want to enlist support, with money, or time, or a vote.

These talks must be more dynamic, more compelling, because action is expected. And what stirs people to act? Involved emotions. Appeal to their emotions.

Before you enter this arena, examine your own feelings. Are you completely in agreement with the principles or the people you represent? Do you feel the program you are supporting is thoroughly worthwhile? Nothing is more obvious than half-hearted support.

A persuasive talker may encounter opponents to his ideas. Some have made up their minds ahead of time; others are doubtful. The latter have come to learn. Their questions may seem contrived, irritating, or downright insulting. No matter how they are put, you as the speaker must keep your temper. Those already on the opposing side may contribute to your knowledge by opening up new avenues of thought, by leading you to consider further arguments to sustain your idea. Welcome them. Your talk will be stronger next time.

Answer the questions with as much skill as you can. If heckling in the middle of your speech is a problem, console yourself with the fact that most of your audience is with you. Don't descend to the level of the heckler and answer back in the same vein. This is fatal. It's what the heckler wants. Wait until peace is restored, then resume with dignity. In the beginning, try to avoid confrontation with known opponents. Wait until you are sure of yourself as a speaker.

Audience participation is valuable. Throw out questions—easy ones, ones that will invite an answer. Have you watched rabble-rousers or non-conformists build up rapport with their listeners? Key words or slogans, repeated at intervals, with the audience joining in, make them feel part of the program and, sometimes, inspire them to act later.

"We shall overcome" represents the hope of many. Impassioned leaders insert that phrase at appropriate intervals. Impassioned listeners repeat it with hypnotic fervor.

Mussolini's technique for rousing his people was extremely effective. In order to unite them against what he considered their enemy, he made sure they were angry, or at least irritated, before he started to address them. His rallies were held in areas hard to reach, uncomfortable, with no shelters or resting places. Mussolini, himself, was invariably late. By the time he arrived, the crowd was restive, ready to blow up.

It took little more on his part to whip them to a higher pitch of anger, not against him, but at some outside target that really had no connection with the original cause of their unhappiness. Mussolini merely redirected their anger.

Many political speakers concentrate on running down the opposition. While this may lend itself to more picturesque speech, a truly strong promotion emphasizes the superiority of the speaker's candidate. In running down an opponent, the speaker is giving him publicity.

Most people are motivated more strongly with the will to do good. Given a choice, they will follow the man who can suggest a constructive course. When you approach your subject with a desire to persuade, examine it carefully. Present the positive side. Appeal to the higher emotions. Your influence will be more lasting. Remember the old Chinese proverb, "The higher a bamboo grows, the lower it bends."

INSPIRE YOUR LISTENER

At one time, we left inspirational talks solely to professionals. Ministers had a near monopoly.

Russell Conwell, a Philadelphia minister, amassed a fortune of between $6 and $8 million at the turn of the century as the result of delivering one speech more than 6,000 times. His "Acres of Diamonds," now printed for all to read, is still popular.

The average man is always eager to improve himself. His self-confidence needs constant nurturing. Help him.

Your own success need not be international. Most people have no desire to become world-famous. They need assistance to live through an average day, to appreciate their own worth.

Researchers claim we all have an almost immeasurable potential. We use approximately 6% of our abilities, compared with the 100% of a new-born who knows no restraint, no inhibitions. You can make others aware of their self-restrictions.

Many businesses, notably those with large sales forces, send their top men to motivation seminars run by professionals. Other businesses have pep rallies in which sales managers attempt to spur their men on to greater successes. If you don't like people or you lack self-confidence, this is not for you as a speaker.

Dr. David Chigos, president of the Training Corporation of America, runs seminars on weekends for executives all over the country. His groups meet at a nearby resort, far removed from city disturbances. His lectures are informal. His listeners participate constantly. Those who attend are invariably stimulated and develop a greater degree of self-confidence.

Evangelists have a strong influence on their listeners. Why? They appeal to their listeners' emotions. Music and drama are essential background props for these orators. They seldom talk quietly or try to maintain personal dignity. They are dramatists. Their voices range, rising to tremendous heights, sinking to sonorous depths. Their talk is physical with their bodily movements exaggerated. Occasionally, they grasp a Bible. They are so imbued with their message that they forget themselves.

You can fit into this group of inspirational speakers if you are connected with a church, or a business, or a club.

Watch the techniques of the leaders. You will discover that the emphasis in all these meetings is on the listening individual, with a strong appeal to his emotions. No matter how stirring an idea is to these intellects, never forget that under each person's calm exterior are powerful emotional urges and a desire to grow in self-appreciation.

LAUGHTER IS ALWAYS WELCOME

Your reputation as a story-teller among your cronies has led your friends to think you can do as well on a platform. They won't ask you to take over the stage and do a Bob Hope special. They will begin at a less sophisticated level—like introducing a speaker, installing new officers, presenting awards.

This is a great opportunity. You can get your feet wet without having to swim. If they don't ask you, volunteer. Most people regard these occasions as bore sessions, ceremonies that have to be endured for the sake of convention. Prove otherwise. Don't try to take over the spotlight. They'll remember you gratefully, in any case, if you bring lightness and humor to the event. It has been said that a smile is the curve that sets things straight. If you add a smile to a gathering, you will be welcomed again.

Humor is difficult to sustain for any length of time. Content yourself, in the beginning, with brightening your other material. There is a whole chapter devoted to humor. Study it well. You may be able to add happiness to every occasion.

FLATTERY—NO; REALISTIC PRAISE
WILL GET YOU SOMEWHERE

A practical joker once sent off ten telegrams to his friends. "Congratulations," was the complete message. He knew of nothing they had done deserving his praise.

Everyone responded with pleasure. Most of them prefaced their replies, verbal or written, with, "I didn't know you knew, but . . ."

In their opinion, they had all done something praiseworthy. Probably with no expectation of recognition. The praise was, thereby, doubly sweet.

Noticing or remarking on another's activity, from performing the plodding necessities to creating spectacular events, is about the best way to build a reputation. Whose? Yours, most of all; theirs, as well.

Give honest praise. Flattery, like too thick icing on a cake, is indigestible. The recipient who has done nothing to merit public notice will immediately assume you are sarcastic, and you have made an enemy. Anything you say after that will be regarded with suspicion, or, even worse, be completely ignored.

Most events are like flashy cars. While the uninformed will react to the superficial top layer, what makes the car worthwhile is the consistently sturdy power train that keeps it moving. So it is with any organization or meeting.

Be aware. Be sensitive to the less flamboyant. They are the ones who arrange the programs. If you want to spread your influence, this is the hard core you must impress. Let them know publicly that you are conscious of their efforts. Let the audience know, too, who is behind the scenes. Honest appreciation or recognition of hard work should always be given.

Some people feel the only way to rise above others is to push them down. A more effective way is to elevate them. You will rise higher, borne on the tide of approval. Your reputation will be enhanced. Too many people forget to say "thank you." That is a magic key. Why should we teach this to our children, then disregard it ourselves?

ON THE CONTRARY

Why do we react more energetically when we disagree? Probably because it's easiest and requires less thinking. Criticism, rebellion against the status quo, is always popular. People will rally quickly behind an outspoken protester. You can join that circle, and be sure you will be heard.

Is that the way to solve problems? If you have something better to offer, be quick to protest—but also be prepared to present a solution. Honest criticism, followed by a verbal blueprint for improvement, will make you a real leader. The dissenter is necessary, but he has no banner to follow unless he takes the infinitely more difficult step of proposing corrective action. For this, he has to use practical and imaginative thinking to develop a solution.

If you want to protest, be sure of your facts. Nothing will discredit your reputation more quickly than having your listeners discover you have depended upon hearsay, instead of upon reliable evidence.

Name-calling of people or projects can be both apt and witty, but mud thrown is ground lost. And some of the mud sticks to the thrower. You can enter the limelight quickly, but you are the loser as well.

People are needed to point out the results of prejudice, inhumanities, inequalities, and the wrongs of society. But, be sure you are motivated by the pros, not the cons. Base your talks on love, not hate, and they will have a more lasting influence.

Choose your field. Support your ideas. Share your experiences and specialities. Your influence and self-confidence cannot help but grow.

Section III

CONSTRUCTING YOUR SPEECH

7

Your Influence Begins with Your Opening

YOUR brain is clicking away with broad themes. Half-formed sentences drift into your mind. A stack of notes sits before you. A book, newspaper clippings, a magazine article add to the clutter. You have to bring all this material together, select or discard according to the action you desire.

A speaker who influences his listeners LEADS them, from his opening words to his final statement. Here's the way he does it, summed up for you:

L	Latch on to your listeners
E	Explain your purpose
A	Amplify your ideas
D	Dramatize your remarks
S	Sum up and stop

Fit your message into these five areas and you are ready to go.

ARRANGE YOUR MATERIAL

If you have your facts on 3 x 5 slips or cards, you can sort easily. Separate your material into three groups: your introduction, your main arguments, and your conclusion.

At this point, make an outline. Don't be concerned with sophisticated, finished phrases. A solid, obvious arrangement in simple words which works well for you is your aim.

Your introduction covers the first two letters of our formula:

Latch on to your listeners

Explain your purpose

The body of your talk will cover the next two points:

Amplify your ideas

Dramatize your remarks

Ordinarily, four points will be the maximum that your listeners can retain. Dramatizing them effectively will take all the time you have left.

Your conclusion accounts for the last letter in our formula:

Sum up (succinctly) and stop

Suppose you want to influence people to support an amendment to lower property taxes. Here is an example that applies this technique:

Introduction

Latch on: Do you want to lower your property taxes?

Explain: Bill #984, now before the House, will lower taxes for homeowners if we all get out and vote "yes" on our ballots next Tuesday.

Body

Amplification 1

Taxing many organizations, now tax exempt, would bring in approximately $270 million dollars, enabling homeowners to pay substantially less.

Dramatize-Use graphs, comparing taxes collected now with those in the future, if the bill is passed.

Amplification 2

Insurance home offices are tax-exempt in our state.

Dramatize-Quote statistics showing wealth of the insurance companies. Show pictures of expensive insurance company buildings.

Amplification 3

Churches in our city own 7% of the downtown high-value property, of which 3% is in commercially profitable apartments, parking lots, and business buildings.

Dramatize-Graphs or pictures, and statistics.

Amplification 4

Educational institutions are in business in our city, owning theatres, clubs, and residences.

Dramatize-Picture of the Recreation Club owned by Southern College.

Conclusion

Sum up: If these commercial interests were proportionately taxed, an untapped source would bring in so much revenue that the pressure on homeowners would be relaxed.

Stop: Go out and vote for Bill #984 on Tuesday.

WAKE THEM UP

Your first sentence is second only to your last sentence in importance, and as such, should not be decided upon until you have gathered your speech into one cohesive whole.

It must be a "hooker," one which catches your audience immediately. It must be short, simple, dramatic, but above all, significant. Never restate your title.

One speaker on crime fires a gun into the air. Others quote a devastating or surprising statistic. Some mention a celebrity who is connected with the topic. A rhetorical question is a favorite opener. Occasionally, the speaker makes an almost unbelievable prophecy: "Tomorrow, you will be . . . "

A more leisurely opening begins with a narrative. Stories have fascinated listeners long before civilization became sophisticated.

While you are developing your speech, it is just as well to use a working introduction. As you go along, you will find that ideas will develop, your imagination will be stimulated. You may even discover that your original thoughts about the content and organization of your speech will change or slant slightly away from your first conception.

Speeches, articles, stories have, to some extent, a life of their own. When I write, my general purpose is determined. I know the conclusion I am working toward. I select the major issues I want to feature. How they fit together depends upon many factors that appear as I work.

It is, therefore, more sensible to leave the opening remarks to the last stages of the speech development. Then, having made the choice, this is the only part to memorize if it is a one-sentence opener. There may be occasions when circumstances will demand a quick revision, but it is very unlikely.

KEEP THEM AWAKE

Your first few words have presumably caught attention. Be brisk and to the point as you proceed. Let your listeners know what your target is, much as a marksman sets his sights before he fires.

In this segment, you are going to let them know why you, particularly, have something valuable to say at this particular time, in this particular place, to this particular group. Bring them into the picture immediately.

Your introduction is a bridge to the rest of your material, and like all bridges, it is more likely to be strong if it is short. Keep your material directly pointed, simple to understand, and related to your listeners.

A selection of anecdotes can be helpful. Some of our highly paid professional speakers reel off a multitude before they get into the body of the talk. If you have an hour or an hour-and-a-half to cover, perhaps this is acceptable, but people will really prefer to have you stick to your topic. After all, that's what they came to hear.

NAME DROPPING'S NO SIN

Scatter names throughout your talk. While celebrities are fair game, you can add much more interest by mentioning someone your audience is likely to know personally.

This is not particularly hard to achieve. There are innocuous stories that a speaker can call upon. Introduce them this way: "Have you heard ... " or, "Someone mentioned while we were coming here ..." or, "Is it true what I've just been told that ..." You can close the tale with a shrug and the lines, "I guess maybe they've been leading me on, but ..."

To employ this bit of strategy, you must confer with your chairman to know the appropriate names. And above all, be sure the stories cannot be misinterpreted and that there is not even the slightest tinge of malice. This way of handling a situation may require too much experience for a beginner, but keep it in mind.

Frank Curran, former mayor of San Diego, is an expert along these lines. Coming into a group, he notes a few names. As he speaks, he mentions them, with gentle humor.

There are innumerable collections of anecdotes available in libraries. Arranged according to broad subjects, they are invaluable for this sort of material.

Again we underline, emphasize the upbeat. A scandalous story about a well-known figure may prove a point with more emphasis than you could otherwise impart. But drop it—there are laws against this. And unless you were actually present when the great name misperformed, you cannot be sure of the facts. Tell the story if you want, but leave out the name.

If you wish to reinforce your story, quote your source, "In *Sports Illustrated,* last week, I read that . . ."

You can manufacture a situation. "What if Gib Schneelock, your own corresponding secretary, were to tell you . . .?" or, "What would Noah do if he wanted to prevent a population explosion among his animals?"

The possibilities are endless. A name will always perk up your audience, and on some occasions, actually make them think.

COLOR IT LOCAL

People like to hear about themselves, about the places where they live. Five thousand children starving in India is distressing. Told with sympathy and emotion, with an appeal for concrete help in the form of dollars, the story will evoke some response. However, if you describe the plight of little Susie Jones living down the street—she's suffering from malnutrition because her unemployed father cannot provide enough to eat—your audience can identify with the problem. Immediate practical aid results.

So it is with any appeal you make. Bring it into the locale of your audience. Dramatize it. Cool descriptive words will appeal to intellectuals, but emotions and drama excite everyone. Coupled with a feeling of familiarity, you cannot help but keep the attention of your audience.

When you know they are with you, when the way is prepared for them to understand and want to hear more, you are ready to begin the body of your speech. You have influenced them to the point of wanting to hear more.

8

Worthwhile Information Will Influence Listeners

EVERY speech must be arranged in a way that is logical to the speaker, and through his treatment, to the audience.

Begin early to pull your thoughts together. Juggle your facts around to see how they fit, to build a logical flow of ideas. Check each point carefully.

1. Is it really important?
2. Does it deserve separate consideration?
3. Is it a subdivision under something more vital?

You are filling in the amplification and dramatization part of the formula LEADS. Set out those facts you consider important to present. Put together added facts or material that will strengthen or dramatize your point.

Norman Thomas, who ran for President of the United States six times on the Socialist ticket and spoke both as a preacher and a politician at different times, constantly asked himself two questions: "Is that so?" and "So what?"

You can promote your ideas in many ways. As noted before, some speeches leave little choice in their arrangement of ideas, although occasionally even an obvious arrangement can be disregarded and the talk enjoyed.

Not long ago, Janet Chelberg of the San Diego Wheelmen told about her three-month cycle trip around Europe and showed slides. Her projector broke down, and in her haste to put slides in another projector's tray, the careful chronological order was disrupted. Everyone, nonetheless, enjoyed the results and the accompanying comments despite the disorder. In fact, they all had a good laugh at the two presented upside down.

Here are the accepted possibilities in arrangement:

1. One fact after another with no particular one predominant.
2. The most important fact first, followed by others in diminishing order.
3. Build to a climax, saving the most important fact till the end.
4. Chronological or geographical order.
5. Agreeable facts first, followed by dissenting ideas.

Your choice of arrangement may affect the influence you will have upon your listeners.

STRING-OF-BEADS APPROACH

All the ideas are equal in strength. They have no inter-relation, need no logical development. As in a string of beads, each point stands on its own, is complete unto itself, and can be considered individually.

A lot of humorous speakers use this technique, telling story after story, about their wives, or husbands, or mothers-in-law.

When no point in a serious talk stands out as more significant, either to you or your audience, each one must be developed carefully and clearly. Expand upon it. Present details to support or describe your feelings or experiences. Quote an authority, or mention someone who is locally known and respected and who agrees with you, if you can. Back up your hard facts with a story.

A positive statement made clearly and decisively after a short pause, will catch an audience. As you develop your backup statements, your listeners may occasionally lose the thread of your thoughts. They may drift off unintentionally, reminded by your words of something else that is near to their hearts or interests.

Unconsciously, your voice or attitude changes slightly as you begin a "for instance," and even the most inattentive listener is aroused.

Repetition of the salient points in well-chosen, picture-painting words, repetition that is indirect, is helpful.

Winston Churchill favored repetition. Advising the Duke of Windsor, he once said, "If you have an important point to make, don't try to be subtle or clever—use a pile-driver. Hit the point once. Then come back and hit it again. Then hit it a third time—a tremendous whack."

Be prepared to switch your materials around to take advantage of a last-minute incident, a news flash, or perhaps, action taken by some governing body. Watch your audience's reactions. Be ready to expand on any point that seems hard for them to understand.

Enumerate your major points: "The first thing to be considered is . . ." "Secondly, we must remember . . ." "Our third point is . . ." If necessary, repeat your statements for emphasis—but not every time.

If you are successful in your explanations, you will see several people nodding in agreement. In religious or inspirational talks, they may murmur "Amen."

Use visual aids or sound effects to dramatize your statements.

Not many talks fit into the "string of beads" group.

Most of them have a definite outline pre-built into their content.

START WITH A PUNCH

Present your biggest argument first. Fired by enthusiasm with this, your audience may accept all subsequent arguments as equally important.

There is a great deal of merit to this idea, particularly if you do have only one major point to utilize in putting your program across. Using your less important material first may lose some of your listeners who are astute enough to recognize the material is insignificant.

Present your weaker arguments with details and "for instances" that will help to reinforce your major statement. Add statistics, biographical information, or other material that is relevant. Refer back, from time to time, to your first argument.

This type of presentation will assure that what you want most to say will be heard. Most audiences are attentive for your early remarks. Perhaps if you catch their interest with strength and imagination in the beginning, they will be aroused and really listen to what you say further.

Judge, therefore, beforehand, very carefully, who will be listening to you—and if shock treatment is required, this may be the best way to get your idea across, to influence your audiences to listen.

BUILD TO A CLIMAX

Most audiences want to have the stories they hear build up to a dramatic or logical conclusion. A startling or promising opening is followed by the enumeration of factual statements, enhanced by supporting material. Each fact becomes even more vital, until the most important one is reached. When this disastrous, or fantastic, or delightful point is made, a pause will underline it.

Although your audience, in following your path of information, has reached this understanding along with you, they should be given time to digest the result.

Handling your voice well is of greater importance, because the building-up process can be reflected in it. Your last point will be in a firmer, more positive, perhaps slightly louder, perhaps slightly softer tone. Your pauses between words may be greater to underline the significance of your remarks.

If you have ever told the story of "Goldilocks and the Three Bears," you have experienced this type of talk.

In a speech on factual material, the effect is just the same. A talk on population growth can begin with statements about present overpopulation problems. A dramatic ending comes with an example of what will happen if we continue at the present rate of births.

When your audience is stunned or excited, you can pound down again on your concluding remark.

TELL IT LIKE IT WAS

If you're planning to describe a trip or process that requires a certain number of steps, you will have little opportunity to do more than follow the pre-determined route. Your highlights, however, may be irregularly interspersed throughout your narration.

You can refer to them earlier without actually describing them. "We thought that was disastrous, but it didn't compare with our adventures on the night of the opening..." "We enjoyed the antics of the chipmunks, thought they were the friendliest animals, until we met some wandering mules..." Drop back to the straight line of your story, but put in plants or hints of excitement as you proceed.

Even though the story is a simple step-by-step recounting of an adventure, anecdotes and opinions of others will enhance your tale.

All through your talk, relate to your audience. If you

know them personally, you can mention them by name: "Hal Story would sure like the fishing in this stream . . ." "For photographers like Bob Bolam, the opportunities are endless . . ."

Your frame may be rigid, but your handling of the material within the frame must be just as skillful, just as appealing as in any other form of speech.

In describing a process for a group of employees, you can make the talk interesting by deliberately inserting material that is relevant but extra. Including experiences of others as illustrations will give your audience time to digest each step slowly and make them retain the information, as well as enlivening an otherwise possible dull discourse.

WHEN YOUR LISTENER DISAGREES

Speeches made before groups who are known to be critical, even antagonistic, are no arena for a beginner. Here is a situation where tackling one man at a time can build a psychological understanding of how to handle many. You can call this the yes, yes, no, NO formula.

You must first gain the approval of your listener. Make your first statement one with which he agrees. Expand on it, building a basis of acceptance.

Your second argument should be as agreeable as the first. He goes along with you.

If he is still willing to listen, introduce a minor negative argument. Bolster it with examples, statistics, stories—whatever comes to mind.

If he has an open mind, and you have been skillful or lucky in discovering an opening, you can bring in your strongest statement at this point.

For example, you would like your listener to vote for a new hospital bond but you know he is against it. You could assemble your arguments like this:

YES: 1. Our hospital should be up-to-date, using new
            methods of saving lives.

YES: 2. Emergencies will not wait until some later, more convenient or prosperous time.

NO: 3. $3 a year seems a small amount for any individual to pay.

NO: 4. A vote for the hospital bond is vital right now.

Each argument will be dealt with at whatever length is deemed necessary. You can add more arguments if your prospect is not ready for the last and most important idea.

Where you need to influence someone against his opinion or decision, you will have to be strategic in your choice of format. You *can* influence him if your proposition is worthwhile. You must circumvent his opposition and let him see the situation as you do.

MOVE FROM SUBJECT TO SUBJECT WITH EASE

Moving fluently from point to point, from argument to anecdote or example, requires smooth transition. With a speaker, words and phrases are the bridges. And the skill is one we have developed as unconsciously as we have learned our speech patterns. The movement should be meaningful, an outgrowth or natural development from the previous remarks.

"Based on the material we have just discussed, . . ." "As we expected, . . ." "And so it was . . ."—all these fragmented sentences can be used to meet different situations.

Single words or short prepositional phrases are just as effective. They are signals that a change is on its way. "Although," "Notwithstanding," "In addition," "For that reason," are all well-worn introductions to new thoughts.

Perhaps the most overused bridge is "That reminds me." Unfortunately, this crutch seems to justify flagrant abuses—a way to insert an anecdote that may or may not be relevant. The speaker decides a change of pace will keep his audience awake and reaches into his store of lately heard jokes. It works! People wake up from a dull discourse to hear the anecdote.

If you want to go into a completely different situation that is allied to your general theme but has no bearing on what has been said before, you can use the very familiar and acceptable "Meanwhile back at the ranch..." gambit upon which television and radio rely.

As in life, a short, simple bridge will get you on to your next subject more quickly and not obscure the material by being too important in itself.

RAMBLING IS RUDE

No matter how important you are, no matter how fascinating your thoughts may be to you, remember your audience may be less than enchanted. If you have not prepared your remarks, you won't need to inform them. You will betray yourself.

While you should never apologize or point out the gaps in your information, do not assume you know your material well enough to speak off the cuff when a time has been set aside for you, and you are aware of it long in advance. Be ready and organized, and you can spread your influence more easily.

HAVE YOU REALLY MADE YOUR POINT?

Before you appear in public, scrutinize your material. You must be sure there are no ambiguities, that your ideas stand out clear and crisp.

In front of your audience, you may still see a puzzled expression as you proceed. Perhaps your speech should be followed by a question period. Always be sure, however, that time will be available or that no one else has been promised the platform immediately following you.

Having given all the material you planned to present, you are ready to wind up your speech. The contents, if well-chosen and carefully presented, have added weight to your opinions and influenced your listeners concerning the conclusion you are about to state.

CHAPTER

9

Pack Power and Influence into Your Last Sentences

YOU have said all you planned. You have to leave your audience informed, inspired, happy, or eager. Your last few words have great importance. Like the burnished patina on a carefully constructed piece of furniture, they will highlight the work put into the body of the talk.

Some speeches are remembered solely for their last sentences. When Patrick Henry's speech before the second revolutionary convention at Williamsburg was reconstructed 40 years after it was originally given, no one had forgotten the famous finish: "As for me, give me liberty or give me death!"

Make up your mind in the beginning, how you want to leave your audience.

1. Are they to be informed only?

2. Do you want them to act?

3. Would you like them to share your experiences?

4. Are you trying to inspire them?

5. Do you want them to laugh and relax?

No matter what your purpose, your thoughts must come to a smooth conclusion, not just a cessation of words.

Look again at our formula. S stands for "sum up" and "stop!" Bring your thoughts to a logical conclusion and stop. Novices often cannot find a graceful way to finish. This is, perhaps, one other place in your speech where memorizing is valuable.

Lloyd George, prime minister of Great Britain, had his own technique for closings. At the end of his prepared speeches, he invariably wrote, "Call on A.G."

When his aide asked what it meant, he replied simply, "Call upon Almighty God."

This is your last opportunity to influence your audience. Your last sentence, therefore, is the most important.

YOUR TIMING IS ESSENTIAL

A suit by one of Savile Rows' outstanding tailors will look ridiculous if it is too big or too small. So it is in speaking. The speech must fit the time slot.

Clock-watching is a must for a speaker. A half-hour speech that runs into an hour is too long. A two-minute speech that takes five minutes is equally too long. No matter how absorbed your audience is, *don't* go beyond your allotted time period. Better to leave them wanting more than to have even one who can criticize your performance based on time alone.

Finish your talk. Let those go who have other appointments. Then, if requested, you can continue in a small, informal group. Or answer questions if your chairman has no objections.

You can't be sure there will be a clock in position to be seen easily. Even though there is a clock, it may be faulty. Have your own wristwatch.

If it bothers you to glance at it, take it off. Lay it on the lectern. Frankly, I see nothing wrong with a speaker obviously checking the time as he talks. It is, after all, courtesy on his part to be aware of the time.

On occasion, you may decide to shorten your speech. A fidgety audience, too many coughs, may indicate that your listeners are becoming impatient. In this event, cut your talk to as bare a skeleton as you can, and let them leave.

While you are conscious of time and willing to let your listeners know that you are, I don't recommend that you do as one speaker I have heard.

He remarked, "Well, I see I have been talking for ten minutes, and since that's all the chairman said I could have, I'd better sit down." That's like chopping off a finger and forgetting to bandage it.

WHEN INFORMATION IS YOUR ONLY GOAL

A neat way to package the talk, frequently used by speakers, is to return to the thoughts expressed in the introduction. Opening sentences, which outline in brief form the aim of the speech, can be used again.

A talk to the Citizens Committee on tax tips for homeowners may begin:

"If you want to pay lower taxes this year, there are many deductions you may have overlooked."

Your ending could be, "And so you see, if you want to pay lower taxes this year, these are the deductions many citizens overlook."

If your listener wants to follow your suggestions, he can You have no desire to do more than inform him.

ACTION IS WANTED

You want your audience to do something. Tell them

clearly and concisely. Let that be the last thing you say. Make positive, brief statements.

"Vote next Tuesday!"

"Beat Tech!"

"Plant a tree."

"Send a contribution."

We are conditioned as children and military personnel to react to the last command. Frequently, you will find that the material you have presented has impressed your listeners with its reasonableness. As you went along, they were in agreement. But ask them to repeat salient points and they may not be able. They will, however, remember your last suggestion if it is made with strength. And they may even be moved to act upon it! Lose them at the end, and where is your influence?

You can phrase your command as a challenging question. A question goads the listener into thought. And, sometimes, action follows thought.

The question need not be stated as such. It may be implied by the situation that you describe as you end your remarks:

"How many new cities, how much undeveloped land will we need to house the population by the year 2,000?" or, "The population is expected to reach 300,000,000 by the year 2,000. City planners are looking for open space to support that number. But the land they want is disappearing rapidly. They don't know where to look."

If your audience has been hostile, asking rhetorical questions is dangerous. Too often, a heckler will shout a reply that is neither helpful nor accurate. And the effect of your discourse may be lost.

If you have been trying to persuade or convince your listeners to do something, and you feel you have been successful, that the majority have been persuaded, you can end with a simple question. "What are you going to do about it?" You have, of course, already told them what you think they should do.

SHARING AN EXPERIENCE

You are giving more than information when you tell about your travels or your adventures raising chinchillas. You want your listener to share your experience.

How do you do this? You must stimulate his senses. There are at least five of them, remember? Sight, sound, smell, taste, and touch. Try to say something that will arouse his memories.

In a travel talk, for instance, you can end like this, "And so, after two weeks, we were glad to pull that dusty old Ford into the driveway, but we'll never forget our visit to the Big Sur."

There's nothing wrong with that. But then again, there's nothing especially right about it either.

How about: "The afternoon was quiet when we got back. The shrubs and trees that decorate our lawn were green and tailored. But in our minds' eye, we saw the wild sky-scratching points of the enormous pines. We heard the far-off sounds of the crashing waves. We felt the damp, cool breeze as it came off the endless sea. We smelled that heady mixture of pine and brine. Pictures may catch some of the essence of this trip for you, but our album of memories is within."

Appeal to their senses. Make them experience your feelings personally.

INSPIRATION IS THE TARGET

If your speech has been inspirational, you will need to center your finish on your listeners. Underline the *you* in your talk. We have been mentioning this all along, suggesting that it will hold your audience's attention. At this point in an inspirational talk, it is essential.

"You, too, can build your self-confidence. You, too, have the ability to do . . ."

An example illustrating the material you have discussed will be a good closing.

"Joe Sawaya was unsure and worried when he spoke. He hated to give his opinions. But by going to Toastmasters Club, he learned how to speak extemporaneously. Now, he represents his group with ease and eloquence."
What he can do, *you* can do."

Your influence here may be more worthwhile than anywhere else. You can give a man self-confidence and serenity.

LEAVE 'EM LAUGHING

Talks intended to amuse listeners must end on a laugh line. It can be an anecdote or a quip.

Be sure it is relevant, and since it is a punch line, set it off. A slight pause will do that.

You could end a talk on women's liberation with:

"Yes, I'm afraid it's true-(pause)

Behind every successful man is (pause) a surprised mother-in-law."

FINISH WITH STRENGTH

You will often find that a capable, penetrating thinker has developed an excellent theme, but his introduction and conclusion are weak. His strong point is his knowledge of the subject. He is so enthused about it that he fails to understand why he should waste time thinking about an introduction. And the same with his ending.

He may not do anything so obvious as explain, "Tonight, I am going to talk to you about . . ." or end with "That's what happened when we made those investigations."

Still, you will recognize that he knows he has come to an end, and he is at a loss. The final words which he has left to the spur of the moment are useless and meaningless.

The introduction and conclusion are the last parts of the speech to polish. Develop them in a temporary form until you have decided firmly on your main thoughts and assertions. But remember, they are as vital as any part of your talk.

You wouldn't send valuable property in an unsealed envelope. Take time to finish your thoughts with a careful seal. They will reach their destination more securely, and will not lose their strength or your influence.

WHEN YOU'RE FINISHED, STOP

The end of your talk is obvious without having to say so. Your skill with words, with thoughts, can indicate you are summing up. You may make an echo statement, repeating your first one, or a dramatic prophecy. You may ask a question or tell a story reflecting what you have said. You will tell them what to do or what they can do. And then you will sit down!

Try not to signal your departure with the hackneyed "In conclusion . . ." or "Finally, . . ." If, however, those words slip out, be sure you mean them. Sending a signal, then failing to follow up and finish is poor planning and damaging to your reputation.

In the three-part speech outline of "Stand up. Speak up. Shut up.", the last point is well taken. When you are done, don't dawdle. Your influence can be lost as your audience loses patience and stops listening.

THANK YOU—NEVER

Some speakers feel a compulsion to say "thank you" at the end of their remarks. What for? Maybe it's supposed to replace the "amen" so many people tack on to the end of their thoughts.

If your audience has listened to you, they have done so because you had something to offer—something they wanted to hear or, at least, know about. You didn't force them to come. Why should you be grateful for their attention? You have worked to put your material together. Even if they pay you something, you have earned it.

Perhaps you are not easily aroused when a performer or speaker tells you, "You've been a good audience tonight." He intends well, no doubt, but he irritates many. We are not kindergarten children who need to have our behavior assessed. As a speaker, avoid this. If it is not arrogance, it seems that way.

If you wish to be gracious, you can say, "I have appreciated the opportunity to be with you." Smile, and sit down.

IN CAPSULE FORM

When an old preacher was asked how he organized his sermons, he replied, "First, I tell 'em what I'm going to tell 'em. Then, I tell 'em. Then, I tell 'em what I told 'em."

Maybe that's the easiest and most impressive way to get your ideas across, thereby, to influence your listeners.

Section IV

**PRESENTING
YOUR SPEECH**

10 Your Voice Carries Influence

So, the mental work is done. All you have to do is stand on your two feet and talk. But like a piano, your tone, rhythm, and volume are significant. Are your words squeaky or deeply resonant? Is your voice forte when it should be pianissimo? Your voice is as vital as any part of your speech.

Some people can repeat anything with such a wealth of meaning in it that they run the gamut of emotions. Otis Skinner tells a story about Madame Modjeska, an outstanding actress, who was guest of honor at a literary society's dinner in Milwaukee. Her short, Polish recitation, given afterwards, was moving, even though the guests did not understand it. One of them asked for a translation.

Madame Modjeska smiled as she said, "I merely recited the alphabet."

The authority in your voice and your articulation frequently determine for your listeners the validity of your talk. A learned dissertation presented in sloppy English loses some of its strength. A con man, on the other hand, impresses his conquests because his voice builds respect.

There are, unfortunately, a few among us who can never speak well. Dulcet tones are impossible. Hearing difficulties may make voice modulation imperfect. A physical defect can be uncorrectable.

But most people who speak badly do so because they either don't care or have no realization of how unpleasant they sound. A decade or so ago, this was possibly excusable. Today, with our opportunities to hear ourselves on tape recorders, no one needs to be unaware of his voice. Have you heard yourself?

If a tape recorder is unavailable, try talking to yourself in a corner of a room. Your voice will come back to you, and if you listen carefully, you will hear how you sound to others.

Does your voice need improvement?

Speeches are more apt to be successful if we:

1. Keep the tone of our voice pleasing.
2. Articulate with precision.
3. Pronounce every word correctly.
4. Pace our words for clarity.
5. Pause for understanding.
6. Vary the volume and stress.
7. Use dramatic techniques.
8. Let our feelings show.
9. Restrict the amount of reading.

The list, while long, is not formidable. Most of us observe the rules in general conversation. Nervousness, however, may disturb some of our pacing and pausing. Self-consciousness may restrain our dramatic impulses.

A weak voice telling us "Stop" may be overlooked. "Stop" thundered by a deep voice will stop us immediately.

Certainly, a voice carries influence to back up expressed ideas or suggestions.

VOICE TONE CAN BE LEARNED OR IMPROVED

Some people are swayed by the richness of a voice alone, but, generally, your voice should be unobtrusive in itself. Nasal, raucous, uneven, or monotonous voices, and those that are too soft or precise, are unpleasant and may direct attention from the content of the speech.

There are many full-sized self-help tomes available in bookstores and libraries. If your problem is serious, you should consider attending a speech clinic. More than likely, the improvement is only a matter of desire and a little work.

A number of our physical organs must work together to produce speech. The most important are the lungs, the larynx, the throat, and the mouth, and finally, the tongue, lips, teeth, and jaw. These organs develop the power, the pitch, the tone, and the articulation of your voice.

Speaking is a secondary function for all these organs. Speaking must be learned. And it can be learned poorly. Bad habits develop before the individual is aware. Raise your involuntary habits to the level of consciousness, and consider your voice objectively. Then, you can train or retrain yourself where you are weak.

Your nerves and muscles affect all your organs. Let us begin with them. If the nerves and muscles in relation to your speaking organs are taut and tense, your voice will be strained and weak. Relax them. Rotate your head, leaving your mouth slack, your jaw loose. Yawn largely. You can do this politely just before you rise to speak.

Breath control is vital. Deep breathing exercises will enlarge your lung capacity, make it possible for you to vary the strength of your voice, the length of your sentences. You can stress words and phrases with more facility.

Your tonal qualities can be improved by reading aloud five minutes a day. Sheer practice in pronouncing words properly, out loud, will result in rounder tones and better breath control; that is, if you read with concentration on your voice in relation to your subject.

Your vocal cords, two membranes, are contained in your larynx, popularly called your Adam's apple. Physiologists tell us the main function of our larynx is to protect our lungs from external irritations, such as smoke, smog, or cold air.

Air from the lungs pushes against the vocal cords, causing a vibration which forms the original speech tone. This tone may be changed in pitch by muscles that control the tension of the cords and the size of the opening between them.

In the next step upward and out, the sound passes through the larger spaces, the throat, nasal cavities, and mouth, which can be likened to cavernous sounding chambers. Here, the sound is amplified or modified. Harsh or mellow tones are developed. We all recognize these changes when we have colds or nasal congestion.

Generally, vowel sounds give depth or body to your speech. Practice, saying several times daily, your own list of words that are rich in these sounds. Here are a few:

a-Baa, Baa, black sheep
e-Whee! sleep, sleek
i-High in the sky
o-Moan and groan
u-Noon, soon, swoon

While there are other vowel sounds, most of them are harsher and not helpful in developing a rich tone. You may have noticed there is more action in your mouth with these sounds. Try singing them as well as saying them. This will have a lubricating effect upon the resonators.

Say with overemphasis, the following lines:

The dog bayed loud and long at the yellow moon above,
While the rabbits and gophers shivered. 'Twas a sound
    they could not love.

ARTICULATE WITH PRECISION

Most of us have read or memorized Hamlet's famous adjuration to the players about to perform in the castle at Elsinore:

> "Speak the speech, I pray you, as I pronounced it to you, trippingly on the tongue; but if you mouth it as many of your players do, I had as lief the town-crier spoke my lines."

Here again, correct articulation can be developed by effort. Ordinarily, we articulate as we have learned unconsciously from our parents or those around us.

Articulation is largely done by the jaw, tongue, teeth, and lips. While the other parts of the sound system make the voice pleasant, understanding depends upon these terminal parts. You will do well to devote much thought to your ability to use them properly.

Do you have a lazy tongue, a heavy jaw, or slack lips? All these cause slight lisps. Tighten them up with practice sentences, such as "Tommy tore the top of the tent." Overemphasize the "t's." "Peter Piper picked a peck of pickled peppers," is another.

Some people have trouble with a hard "g." They find it difficult to say words like "singing," or combinations like "Long Island," without tripping over their tongues. Or they end their words with a "d" sound instead of a "t." "Get out" becomes "ged oudt."

Missing teeth, of course, affect these sounds.

Have you heard about the missionary who sent his dentures off to be repaired? After a long wait, he was finally rewarded with their reappearance.

Popping them into his mouth, he said with great fervor, "Jesus Christ! Jesus Christ!"

His wife, shocked at her husband, remonstrated.

"Honey," he whispered, "I haven't been able to say that without whistling for ten years."

Most of us have problems from time to time. General well-being is the first and most important consideration. None of us are efficient when weary or weak as the result of colds or the aftermath of more serious illnesses.

Examine your speech by means of a recorder if possible. Listen objectively. Tidy up your articulation. Discover and remove mannerisms that can be irritating. But above all, when you know you are to deliver a talk, be sure you are rested and alert.

Listeners can forgive many inadequacies, but you owe it to yourself and them to be physically at your best.

PRONOUNCE EVERY WORD CORRECTLY

If we cannot correct physical problems, we can, at least, be sure we are pronouncing words properly.

I won't forget listening to a local doctor who was an authority on car safety. He had delivered an untold number of lectures on the subject. One word, he used over and over again: "pan-ay-sha." Every time he said it, it was like being hit. I lost the thread of his theme each time. The word, of course, was "panacea" (pan-a-sée-a).

His reputation did not suffer in this case, but certainly his listeners were jolted.

Dictionaries are not expensive. Even if you have not studied phonetics, you can understand their explanations. There are large, comprehensive volumes such as *Webster's New International*. There are pocket-sized versions. One of the best desk dictionaries is *Webster's Collegiate Dictionary*.

If you must use slightly unusual words, be sure to check them. You may even be a shade off in your interpretation.

There are a few words commonly mispronounced. "February" frequently loses its first "r." Athletes become "ath-a-letes" and larynx becomes "larnyx." Bronchial tubes are "bron-i-cal." This is sheer sloppiness and should be avoided by anyone who is seriously interested in speaking to the public.

Place names can vary. In our locality, we have a town called Poway. Everyone has his own idea of the correct pronunciation. The Himalaya Mountains and the Caribbean Sea have distressed purists for many years. Whatever you use is probably acceptable, but if there is a question, explain to your audience that you have decided to use one specific pronunciation because there is no apparent "right" way.

We do not always realize we are mispronouncing words, but when we are doubtful, we must consult a dictionary.

PACING IS PERTINENT

Just as vital as sound is to our speech is silence. Long silences we know as pauses. But that infinitesimal silence between words is even more important.

The average man talks at a rate somewhere between 120 and 180 words a minute. The subject and audience determine the pace. Obviously, technical subjects must be developed slowly. Kindergarten children need time to understand instructions. Bob Hope's patter, however, would lose much of its effect if not presented swiftly.

Not long ago, I sat in an audience and listened to a talk on faith healing. It wasn't long before I was completely lost. The torrent of words came too fluently. The sound went up and down like a wave. The effect was musical, but only with severe concentration was I able to pick out individual words. It sounded almost like a Latin chant.

The mystery was solved when I heard, later on, that the man had been a priest for many years.

Pace varies with content. A broadcaster describing a horse race or tennis match must speak quickly. His listeners would be annoyed by perfect, complete sentences.

In fact, speaking is an art that does not go by the strict rules of grammar. Fragmented sentences are often more dynamic. Like music, rhythm is vital for interest. Long sentences covering long thoughts should be interspersed with short sentences or phrases.

If you are nervous, you tend to speak rapidly. Relax. Slow down deliberately. You are going too quickly if you notice frowns of effort. If you don't slow down, those frowns will disappear because their owners have stopped trying to understand.

Don't slow down to the point of seeming weary. You can be enthusiastic and strong at a slower pace.

Consider the old master, Winston Churchill. No one would accuse him of being lukewarm on any subject. His tone was strong, but he never hurried. Think about some of his words delivered at a conversational pace.

"I have nothing to offer but blood, toil, tears, and sweat."

Would that famous line have had any power delivered quickly in a light voice?

PAUSE FOR UNDERSTANDING

Pauses are powerful aids if properly used. They allow people time to digest what has been said. They also act as silencers, preparing the way for important statements, ones that should not be lost or overlooked.

Churchill was noted for his "pregnant pauses." Where other speakers stressed words or phrases by volume of sound, Churchill relied upon silence.

The story goes around that at one time, he paused for four minutes. When asked about it afterward, he admitted that he had lost the thread of his thoughts. He had had to review mentally his complete talk before he could continue. So great was his reputation, however, that his audience remained silent, thinking deeply, we hope, on the points he had made up until then.

For that is what the pause is supposed to do: allow

listeners to contemplate what has been said, to rearrange their thoughts in silence to meet the thoughts of the speaker.

Jack Benny uses pauses or "double takes" constantly in his routines. Almost invariably, the spot gives his audience time to laugh, to catch up with his jokes.

One kind of pause every speech can do without is the nervous "er" or "ah" novices insert. No sound at all is better than that. Young people and those lacking confidence have a tendency to use "you know" as a crutch. This is their way of establishing a form of rapport. But it, too, acts like a hurdle on a straight course to understanding.

Consider your speech. Is there something so important that you want it to be heard, to be thought about? Pause. Pause noticeably, both in speech and movement.

Strangely enough, issues gain in their emphasis—not through a spate of words but by standing alone, clear-cut, as a beautiful diamond glows more brilliantly when placed alone on a simple square of black velvet.

VARY YOUR VOLUME AND STRESS

When I consider other languages of the world, I am thankful that English is my mother tongue. Despite its unusual twists, pronunciations, and grammatical inconsistencies, it does not carry with it the added burden of words meaning something quite different according to the key in which they are spoken.

But there is no excuse for speaking in a monotone. Few of us do in general conversation. Yet many, when called upon to speak in public, try to be too correct. The result is dull and without personality.

Words have color in themselves. Some are explosive, others gentle. Words with "p's", "b's", or "t's" have staccato effects, whereas "s's" and "l's" have soothing, calming cadences. When you use them, give them the benefit of their characteristics. Articulate carefully.

Change in volume is perhaps the easiest way to vary our

sound, but there is no need to shout. I have heard one preacher work himself into such an emotional fervor that his words rang out with a deafening blast. He assaulted our ears and detracted from his message. Raise your voice, of course, but keep it within normal limits.

Whispering, on the other hand, is effective in many situations. Teachers use this as a device to bring a group to attention. But the group must be small.

Whispering within a talk is not necessarily an indication of intimacy. A stage whisper can carry amazing distances. Walter Hampden, one of our century's most distinguished actors, was an expert. Dropping your voice in the middle of a discourse highlights the point being made.

Stress of individual words often changes the meaning of the sentence. Any simple three-word sentence can serve as an example. Try "You are sick."

You are sick. You *are* sick. You are *sick.*

We have remarked before that emotions are important. Let them show in your voice when you speak. If you hate something—a form of injustice, irresponsibility—let your listeners know. If you love something—a selfless action by someone, a beautiful place, a spiritual writing—be willing to share your feelings. Joy transmits quickly. Sadness and unhappiness will reach your audience equally fast.

The overall mood of pessimism or optimism will pervade almost any speech. Mostly, this will be unconscious. If you see no way out of a problem, perhaps pessimism is justified. But, generally, think about your subject, and try to find the bright side or, at least, a possible solution—particularly if you want your audience to correct the situation.

Most of the time, the difference between an optimist and a pessimist is only the point of view. Where an optimist will be happy because a glass is half full of water, the pessimist, seeing the same glass, will be distressed because it is half empty.

DRAMATIC TECHNIQUES ARE EFFECTIVE

Be dramatic if you can, but not obviously so. Don't discuss the devastating effects of a hurricane in the same tone as for a light breeze. Don't mention mortality statistics cheerfully. Your audience won't expect a fluttering handkerchief, but a certain amount of dignity or solemnity is demanded.

If you feel your voice needs more variety, that it needs loosening, practice will help.

A parent with young children can go "way out" telling the story of Goldilocks and the three bears. The only thing wrong with this is that the children will be so delighted that their demands for a repeat will be more insistent.

Some poems have tremendous possibilities. "The Barrel Organ" and "The Highwayman" are two excellent poems by Alfred Noyes. They are full of color words and opportunities for variety in pitch and pace. Tennyson's "Song of the Brook" is another one, easily found, and providing opportunities to dramatize:

> I come from haunts of coot and hern
> I make a sudden sally,
> And sparkle out among the fern
> To bicker down a valley ...
>
> I chatter, chatter, as I flow
> To join the brimming river,
> For men may come and men may go,
> But I go on forever.

There are many poems that can be used to give you a feeling for drama, that can help you vary your voice. And it's lots of fun to read them out loud to yourself. Try it!

LET YOUR FEELINGS SHOW

Your personality is the keystone on which all your other traits and abilities are developed. You don't have to tell anybody you're a good guy. Forget yourself when you speak. Concentrate on your subject, but let your personal character- istics shine through. Don't try to assume an attitude you feel is false.

We have concentrated in the beginning of this chapter on ways to use your voice, thinking about pauses, stresses, pitch, pronunciation. They should be considered. Then, drop them back into your subconscious, and let them come forth naturally. However, don't try to squelch your natural feelings: indignation, joy, reverence, sincerity, disgust, pride. There is no gimmick, no technique that can be taught, to compare with natural expression.

An elderly speech teacher of mine insisted that we could not communicate any real emotion unless we had our minds concentrated solely on our subject. Repeating words we had memorized could only be empty words artificially delivered.

SHOULD YOU READ?

Do you not trust yourself without a printed page in front of you? No matter how well you read, it shows. There is a lack of spontaneity. Listeners are willing to accept reading when it comes to news commentaries on television or radio where timing is essential. But what is your excuse?

Is your talk so tightly scheduled that a minute or two one way or another matters so much? Is your subject so rigid that it cannot bend to the needs of the moment, to the needs of the people who are listening?

Some speakers memorize their talk. Don't! That's just another form of reading—reading from within your brain, but reading nonetheless. If you miss a key word, you are apt to stumble and the talk may dissolve into a shambles for a moment or two, if not altogether.

If you must write down your speech in its entirety for purposes of timing or even to get the points worked out in a logical flow, that's acceptable, but not recommended.

Written-out speeches tend to be essays, not talks. The

vocabulary is different. Reading is slower-paced and can be re-read for clarification. Unfortunately, most of us become so enamored with our prose that we tend to revert to it even if we are making a conscious effort to speak freely.

One speaker told us that he felt he was not doing his best when he spoke extemporaneously on a pre-assigned subject. He decided to devote more time to write out his thoughts. After several experiments, he had to admit that, while the talk looked exciting and polished on paper, it was as dull as yesterday's news. He gave up the extra work and prepared only a skeleton.

Certainly you should be prepared. You will have thought out your arguments carefully. You have outlined them somewhere.

Most speakers have notes. The better, more accomplished ones seldom refer to them. Here is where small 3x5 cards are invaluable. They can be put away inconspicuously in a pocket or purse, and later be rested lightly on the edge of the lectern.

Write out your opening line if you think stage fright will envelop you—but that's all! Key words after that should be sufficient to keep your talk pointed where you want it to go. It is wise to have this, at least, because you can then be sure you have not, in your enthusiasm for one idea, overlooked another. A quick glance will suffice to restimulate your thinking, reactivate your memory.

Exceptions to this policy are quotations and statistics. Those, I always write out. You may choose to use a broad number as you speak, "Around 50,000 people . . ." But you may be questioned later. It is well to be able to say, "According to the *World Almanac,* 50,985 people . . ." Or use that figure in your talk and refer to your notes for assurance. Your listeners will respect your effort to be correct unless you use a crutch too often.

Statistics can be very dull, and too much emphasis on insignificant, fine details will weaken interest in the broad theme.

Quotations are tricky. You may have used one all your life, but there, on the public platform, it can desert you completely. Write it out.

Use your notes only if necessary. It is amazing how seldom you will need to refer to them if you have them with you. Not only will you remember what to say, you will have a picture of your notes in your mind which, in itself, is a memory jogger.

Your concluding statement, particularly if it is a startling one, perhaps should be written out and memorized. Whatever you do, don't fumble it.

Your family may be impressed with your reading of Bible verses, your dramatic recitations from Mother Goose, but leave that talent at home. When you are asked to talk to people, talk to them as people.

BUT, NEVERTHELESS

You can break every rule in the book, probably not all of them at the same time, and still be successful. If your thoughts are "on fire," if you honestly put your audience before yourself, you cannot help but influence your listeners.

Lincoln's nasal tones, his awkward gestures, casual dress, never deflected from his innate sincerity. He had something to say, and he said it without sophistication or polish. His thoughts were clear; his feelings were evident; he made his point!

English speech, according to Lord Birkett, writing in the *Oxford Book of English Prose* is "as malleable and pliant as Attic, dignified as Latin, masculine, yet free from Teutonic guttural, capable of being as precise as French, dulcet as Italian, sonorous as Spanish."

You have the vehicle in which to express yourself and every emotion that can stir you.

After you have practiced and learned the techniques, forget them on a conscious level. Think of what you are saying. Think deeply. Your subconscious will bring forth the appropriate physical ways of expressing these thoughts. Your listeners, aware of your deep conviction, cannot help but be affected by your beliefs. Your influence will be felt.

11 Gestures Strengthen Ideas that Influence

YOUR listeners are watching you. Give them something to look at. Gestures are a natural outgrowth of our thoughts and communication.

No one needs to tell a child how to emphasize his thoughts with action. In fact, he begins with action. If he doesn't like his cereal, he dumps it. Everyone understands. If he likes his companion, he puts out his arms in a universal expression of love that transcends any language barrier.

On the public platform, however, this uninhibited baby, grown to adulthood, is apt to freeze. And the absence of natural movement is more obvious than overactivity.

Your movements strengthen your words. Strong, sweeping gestures can accompany strong, sweeping statements.

At one time elocution lessons were in vogue, and teachers assigned specific actions to memorized words. Today, we emphasize natural activity.

Be sure that:

1. The gesture matches the thought.
2. The gesture can be seen.

Gestures are sign language used or understood, consciously and unconsciously, by everyone who can see.

1. Going to the lectern, we exhibit enthusiasm or dignity by our approach.
2. Our posture at the lectern shows our mental and emotional attitude.
3. Faces, particularly eyes, are telltale evidences of sympathy, indignation, anger—all the emotions.
4. Hands alone can convey a message when speech fails.

Raise your awareness of your present gestures to the level of consciousness. Discover what you are doing. Correct any awkward or half-hearted movements. Omit irritating or disturbing habits. Then, let yourself go. Your words of influence are doubly strong.

MAKE YOUR FIRST IMPRESSION POWERFUL

No matter what the chairman has said about you, your audience will begin to judge you personally from the moment you stand up. We depend more upon our eyes than our ears for many impressions. And that first impression is hard to alter.

Are you poised? Do you walk with confidence? Are you hesitant, nervous, clutching an untidy mass of papers? Is your tie straight, your hair combed? If you're a woman, your hat should be an ornament for your face, not an attraction in itself. Make sure your clothes are comfortable, particularly your shoes. Avoid jewelry which is distracting.

If you're coming in from the side or up from the front, show your enthusiasm. Walk briskly as though you are anxious to start. If you're at the head table, rise with obvious pleasure and a smile upon your face. You're happy to be there.

Occasionally, the type of talk or welcome you have received will call for a running entrance, such as pep talks at football rallies. Other times, you may have a fanfare and be expected to make a fairly impressive entrance. But this is not often.

When you are safely in front of the lectern, wait for a few seconds. Survey your audience with warmth. Put your notes and your watch (if you feel it necessary) where they are available but not obtrusive.

You're ready to start. These are the people you are going to influence!

STAND AT EASE

You want to concentrate on your ideas. Stand so that you are comfortable. You won't need the rigid military bearing of a West Pointer, but stand as straight as you can.

The Tokyo Police Department believes this. In a handbook for their men, in 1959, they wrote: "Always stand at attention when you are telephoning; otherwise, your slouch will show in your voice."

Have your weight centered somewhat forward. This presents an appearance of eagerness. Leaning back too far suggests aloofness. You *are* enthusiastic about your material, aren't you? Let your whole body cooperate in your delivery.

Whatever you do, be energetic enough to stand without help. Leaning on a lectern may seem a casual stance to you. To your viewers, you look tired or sloppy, and the enthusiasm you are trying to engender won't happen. They take their cue from you. If you are weary, they are either embarrassed to have taken your time or they will reflect your seeming lack of excitement in your subject.

You don't have to stand still. Your notes won't run away. You can move to one side or the other, particularly if you are not at a table, although it's quite all right to do so even then. A fixed microphone may restrict your movement, but you can turn your body sideways, always remembering to speak into the mike.

The movements you make can support your message. Move forward as you make a point. Retire a step or two as you finish your argument. If you have been especially dramatic, this is a cue to your listeners to take a breath, relax, then be ready for your next assertion.

These movements are all natural. Watch yourself objectively as you discuss something with your friends. If you are on your feet, you will find yourself moving forward to underline an important remark, stepping back with a shrug if it isn't.

Some of us have "natural" bad habits that must be overcome. I have trouble with my feet. Unless I work at it, I find myself rising up and down as I make each point. Others sway from side to side. This does nothing but distract an audience. You can, however, overcome these tendencies, to some extent, by placing one foot in front of the other before you start.

Discover what you do wrong. Your family will be delighted to tell you. Try to overcome disturbing movements, but above all, relax. A spotlight, literal or figurative, is not hold-fast glue!

LOOK AT YOUR LISTENERS

Who are you talking to? Whoever they are, you should look at them. One to one, you wouldn't avoid their eyes. Why should you do so just because there are more listening to you?

Pick out those who seem to be congenial, in different sections of the room. If someone seems to be having difficulty following your ideas, single him out for attention. You will slow down, perhaps, until his worried frown disappears. If one of your listeners keeps whispering to a companion, talk to him directly for awhile. He'll stop his disturbing chatter, and his friend will undoubtedly be grateful to you. He came to hear you, not his friend.

Don't stare at a spot a foot or two above your audience's heads. That's chatting with the angels, and you're not practicing for that eventuality yet. If you're on television, chat with the camera. You can look away occasionally to break the monotony.

Reading makes eye contact more difficult, which is just one more reason not to read. Larry Sweeney, evaluating at a Toastmaster meeting, complained after a member read his speech. "There were three things wrong with your speech: one, you read it; two, you didn't read it well; and three, it wasn't worth reading in the first place."

Be natural. You are talking to people, not just expounding your views to a number of filled seats.

Face mobility is vital. Some comedians, like Buster Keaton, have earned their livings by keeping their faces frozen. Unless you are striving for a comic or some other dramatic effect, that's not for you.

Let your face reflect your emotions: joy for the future, disgust with unnecessary despoliation of nature, enthusiasm for your hobby, concern for the hungry. If your emotions are obviously involved, your appeal will stimulate your listeners more powerfully than your words!

HANDY HINTS

Those appendages from our shoulders are the most troublesome components to handle. People actually have taken up smoking or drinking to occupy their hands in difficult situations. Ladies flutter handkerchiefs; men adjust their clothing continually. Anything, just anything, to keep their hands busy.

If you are the kind who waves your arms at the slightest incident, go ahead. If you are the reserved type, you won't introduce windmill swings into your talk, but do loosen up, rather than tighten up. Your motions should be there, as part of your talk, not laid on as an extra.

Consider how universally understood are many of the movements we make without thinking:

1. We point. This clarifies or segregates a thought from the mass, or very simply, shows a direction.
2. We hold out our hands, palms up. We are giving or receiving something, or we're wondering about it.
3. We hold our palms down. We are rejecting an idea.
4. We clench our fists. Even the less pugnacious use this gesture to show their anger, disgust, or irritation.
5. We raise our palms with our fingers pointing straight up. All over the world, that means stop. We disapprove of the idea we have just discussed.
6. We cut the air with our hands. We mean a division of some sort.
7. We draw imaginary pictures. For a circular staircase, a Roman candle, we weave spirals in the air. We show shapes and sizes, from pretty girls in bikinis to the fish that got away. We show how a kite swoops, a diver performs a jackknife, a golfer drives one straight down the middle.

When words or meanings fail us, .we resort to pantomime. Travelling around Europe, we often used our hands when our words were meaningless. Results can be gracious or belligerent.

My teenage son made a peace sign not too long ago and had to depart quickly. His casual gesture at a local beach stirred immediate anger on the part of three close-cropped young men.

Hand signs often become personalized. No one will forget Winston Churchill's "V for Victory" sign, two raised fingers. Eisenhower, younger and less restrained, flung his arms wide in a "V" sign.

Hands clasped in front of them, Orientals welcome you. Mexicans waggle their fingers "no" instead of their heads, and everyone understands their meaning.

Not using your hands or arms is almost worse than using

them awkwardly. Have you not been impressed by the limp arms of Irish dancers as they go through complicated foot patterns?

Your hands are alive. They have a purpose. Use them well, not as flopping, half-caught birds, but as free, soaring additions that add color and power to your words.

FROM HONOLULU TO ROME, BODY TALK IS IMPORTANT

The Hawaiians make their "body talk" more a matter of romance set to music. They say the hands are doing all the talking.

No face-to-face communication is complete without movement—movement of every part of the body. Watch strangers in the street. Many times you will be able to "listen in" on their conversation without hearing a syllable.

Italians are supposed to be the most energetic of speakers. Minor accidents in that country bring into view most dramatic reactions: flailing arms, clenched fists, glaring faces. A crowd collects, and in no time at all, they have cheerfully joined in the argument. Gestures fill the air. Everyone is enjoying himself.

Your own personality will determine the extent or number of gestures. Consider the movie personalities. Jack Benny is restrained and slow; Milton Berle is loose and active; Jerry Lewis, at times, seems boneless, and in some of his most inspired moments, completely disjointed.

No matter how skilled and serene you are, speaking stimulates your adrenal glands. Physically, you are ready to go into battle. If you don't move, this excess energy may make you tense.

And you are not the only one who is tense. Your audience will reflect your physical attitude if you are communicating well. Your moving will relax them, too. On the conscious level, they are not aware of this, and neither should you be. But do not try to tone down or omit natural actions.

MATCH ACTION TO WORDS

Whatever you do, be sure your action and your words come out even.

There once was a preacher who said, "When the call comes from up yonder" (with his arm raised high and pointing), "I'll be there." (but his arm had dropped too soon!).

In "Uncle Sam wants *you*," be sure you're pointing when you get to the key word. Begin your gesture in advance, but time it accurately.

Generally, actions that raise your arms above your shoulders imply inspiration or uplift. Those at shoulder level indicate calmness or serenity. Those below the shoulders denote rejection or a negative feeling.

Before the advent of the microphone, gestures were vital. The people on the fringes of the crowd could often follow the speaker more through his actions than his words.

Some of our more famous orations ended dramatically with unforgettable pictures that have lived through the years.

William Jennings Bryan ended his famous "Cross of Gold" speech with, "You shall not press down upon the brow of labor this crown of thorns. You shall not crucify mankind on a cross of gold."

As he spoke those words, he held an imaginary crown in his hands, the fingers spread inward as thorns. Slowly, he brought it down onto his head, close to his temples. Then, with his last sentence, he held his arms straight out at right angles, signifying the cross. He stood silently for five seconds, then stepped back. He was almost at his seat before the hypnotized audience broke the silence.

He did not know why he had the effect he did upon his listeners. He had no contrived gestures. He was "on fire" with his thoughts. He was so wrapped up in them that he forgot himself and was completely natural.

Patrick Henry, the fiery Virginia delegate, was flamboyant in his gestures.

William Wirt reported that as Henry said, "Give me liberty or give me death," he held up an ivory letter opener in his hand. When he came to the word "death," he brought the opener down so that it appeared to sink slowly into his breast.

Patrick Henry was not a pre-possessing figure nor very popular among his colleagues, but his close emotional involvement with the issues he supported gave him a stature and influence far beyond others.

THE MAIN POINT

When you are enthused about your subject, you will convey that enthusiasm as much through your physical actions as your words. Remember that your audience is watching as much as they are listening—maybe more so!

There are about 600,000 meaningful gestures according to one expert. Surely you can find suitable ones to dramatize your words.

Your influence will be magnified.

12 Words Alone Have Influence

WORDS have power in themselves. Your ideas must be clothed in words that are not only understandable but appealing and positive.

When you are organizing your speech, try out phrases and words on those around you. Watch their reactions. Some words are irritating; some are ambiguous.

Is a man garrulous or a windbag? There's a difference, although the dictionary meaning is the same.

In a speaking vocabulary, there are a few guide rules:

1. Strive for simplicity.
2. Use familiar terms and concepts.
3. Accents, if natural, are acceptable; if artificial, they are dangerous.

4. Slang is seldom necessary or attractive.
5. Avoid obscenities because they are so strong in themselves that they tend to diminish thoughts they are meant to convey. And many listeners are offended.
6. Be creative in your phrases and sentences. Find original word combinations.
7. Use picture-painting words to stimulate the senses.
8. Positive, optimistic words are more appealing and frequently more enduring.

Choose the best possible words to cummunicate ideas. They are the vehicles carrying your thoughts to your listeners. Influence depends first upon understanding.

SIMPLE WORDS ARE ALWAYS PREFERABLE

What are simple words? Rudolf Flesch, one of our country's leading authorities on communication, says, "Simple English is no one's mother tongue. It has to be worked for."

Occasionally, there are five-syllable words that are better than one- or two-syllable words. There are a few recognized or used by everyone. Many have no exact synonyms. But who said you are limited to a word rather than a simple sentence?

"Ubiquitous" is a lovely word. I remember the first time I heard it: "The ubiquitous sparrow broke the morning silence with its cheerful call." Can you guess its meaning from the sentence? I couldn't. Was it grey, or noisy, or flying, or happy? Replacing it with "omnipresent" makes the meaning clear, but it, too, is a less used and pretentious word.

Why not just say, "There were sparrows, as usual. They broke the morning silence . . ."

This does not mean talking down to an audience. Not everyone has the same background. Even an Einstein would probably be at a loss at a fashion designers' gathering.

If your ideas are complicated, there is a greater need for simple words.

Winston Churchill once remarked, "The short words are the best, and the old words are the best of all."

Classic examples from his speeches show us the power of simplicity:

"We shall fight in France. We shall fight in the seas and oceans. We shall fight in the air. We shall defend our island whatever the cost may be. We shall fight on the beaches; we shall fight on the landing grounds; we shall fight in the fields and in the streets; we shall fight in the hills. We shall never surrender."

"I have nothing to offer but blood, toil, tears, and sweat."

"An Iron Curtain has descended across the Continent."

Is there a better way to say it? Maybe. But his message could not be misunderstood by his listeners.

FAMILIAR WORDS ARE MORE MEANINGFUL

Simple words are not always understandable. See if you recognize these: gusset, sedum, cryogenics, braise, nihilistic, plimsoll. If you know the meaning of all those words, you're a word-collector, perhaps a crossword-puzzle fan. Yet, they are all simple, much-used words for some people.

The average man would be at a loss. There is no such thing as an average audience. Your vocabulary has to be selected with each specific audience in mind. Realize that photographers and doctors define "diaphragm" differently; investors and school teachers have their own interpretation of "margin."

If you have any doubt about your audience's background, take time to explain specialized words and phrases. Let them understand what you want them to do.

ACCENTS ARE ACCEPTABLE

If you have an accent, don't worry about it. Enthusiastic speech will overcome any unusual pronunciation or misplaced idiom. In fact, a legitimate accent often adds to the acceptance of the information, even though the reputation is undeserved.

For example, a Frenchman talking about sauces will carry more weight than an American, even though the latter is known to be a better cook. Germans are respected for their scientific knowledge; Italians for their romance. In this country, when a Southerner speaks in favor of integration, he has greater impact.

Occasionally, you may want to tell a story about a national or racial group. A little accent may add interest, but keep it as brief as possible. Affecting an accent can alienate the listener, who may interpret a slur where none was intended.

Foreign words or phrases can be used, but sparsely. Too many people do not recognize them. And while some may be impressed by your great knowledge, just as many may be disenchanted by what seems to them affectation.

A few Yiddish words in a Jewish audience may establish rapport; one or two Scots' words at a Burns celebration are acceptable, but simplicity is your most important consideration.

Don't lose any listeners by being too sophisticated or humorous at the expense of others.

SLANG IS UNNECESSARY

Do you really know the slang of today? It changes so rapidly. From time to time, the meanings completely reverse themselves. One obvious example is "square." In the thirties, everyone wanted to be thought of as "square." A "square deal" was the best to be had.

In the sixties, a tone of derision accompanied the title "square." Anyone who was "square" lacked imagination.

There is something absurd about an adult who resorts to slang. That's perhaps why comedians often use it.

One lady in New York frequently used the slang her children brought home. At that time, and in their school, biology classes were called "bugs." When her teenagers talked about "bugs," the word went unnoticed. When she used it, the word grated. If anything, she made the generation gap more obvious.

Don't resort to slang to be "with it." Your front will be pierced easily by the users, and the suspicion arises that you are talking down to them.

Besides, there is nothing so monotonous as slang. The words stand out like pickets on a fence, bobbing up at intervals, cutting off the view, or, in this case, your thoughts from your listeners.

SOME WORDS SHOULD BE AVOIDED

Four-letter swear words or obscenities are shockers. If they are used infrequently, they are dynamite when tossed into an otherwise sober, conventional speech.

One student rioter was taped for television at a large student rally. His harangue was so loaded with obscenities that the authorities were unable to broadcast more than a few sentences of his speech. The picture came through, but the young man lost the opportunity to communicate with a larger, previously unreached audience. Which meant he lost the opportunity to influence all those listeners.

A respected nutrition expert sprinkles swear words throughout her discourses. She turns a lot of potential followers away, who become so indignant at this habit that they miss the message.

Beyond the four-letter words are others that embarrass many listeners. Consequently, a whole new vocabulary is introduced. We can call it a "veneer" vocabulary since it merely puts a dressy surface on an old structure.

Who wants to live in the slums? For years, authorities called buildings there "substandard dwellings." A reverse psychology made "ghetto" acceptable. Poor people are the "underprivileged" or "disadvantaged." Somehow, this takes the sting out of the condition.

All through our society, we gloss over occupational titles. Trash men are "sanitary engineers"; janitors are "custodians." Children who do badly in school are called "underachievers." Are there "overachievers?" No, they are called "gifted children."

Ladies no longer "dye" their hair. "Tint" sounds so much better. The bathroom has so many synonyms or symbols that people are frequently at a loss. Take, for example, the young Easterner visiting the West for the first time.

After excusing herself delicately from the restaurant table, she returned to ask her escort, "Am I a mare or a stallion?"

Watch your choice of words. Reserve the power of the four-letter ones for something important. Choose words that will not offend. The English language is so filled with synonyms, with many ways of explaining difficult concepts, that the man who can only call a spade a spade probably deserves one. Influence comes when listeners are appreciated and not offended.

BE ORIGINAL

You're a new person with new experiences. Find your own way to describe the action. Build a present-day picture for your listener. "Sly as a fox," "looking for a needle in a haystack," "pleased as Punch" are ideas from the past or a foreign place. Few know anything about foxes; even fewer have personally been involved with a haystack. How many know Punch is an excitable puppet well-known to British moppets? Use phrases that are related to your generation and environment.

Back in 1783, Jonathan Swift collected and published a volume he called *Complete Collection of Gentle Conversation— Now Used in the Best Companies of England.* He assured his readers that every one of the phrases that were included had been in use for more than 100 years. With "tongue in cheek," he implied that the clichés were examples of great wit. The terrible thing about the whole collection is that, now, 200 years later, these phrases are still bouncing around, still keeping people from experiencing the joy of their own creativity.

Catchy phrases and sharp, new pictures that relate to them will be more challenging.

Watch out for crutches, for favorite words. From President Nixon's "I want to make perfectly clear . . ." and President Kennedy's "vigor," comedians have created many hilarious skits. A number of amateur speakers tuck in the word "hopefully" as a bridge between ideas. One minister thoroughly upset one of his parishioners because he overused the word "individuals" when "people" or "persons" would have varied his text.

Surely you recognize the more obvious crutches favored by many. Try to avoid them if you can. Here are a few:

As you well know
Each and every one
Words fail to express
In the last analysis
Beggars description
Make a motion
Venture to make a suggestion
At a loss for words
With no further ado
Do justice to the occasion
Goes without saying
Last but not least

Adjectives are often frozen onto some nouns. Crowds are almost invariably "motley." Silence is "discreet" when it doesn't "reign supreme." "Slippery" is usually tied in with eels or banana peels. Can't you think of something else that's slippery? How about a drop of mercury, or a peeled grape?

Trite expressions with a twist are acceptable—more than acceptable. They have the ability to arouse your listeners, because, ordinarily, they will have ended the phrase for you in their minds. When you end it differently, a small shock results.

He who laughs, lasts.
A company is known by the men it keeps.
Hear today, gone tomorrow.

Think of your speech as a lawn covering a large area. How much more attractive it will be with patches of color. These patches are the original phrases, the unexpected turns of wit that you insert.

WORDS CREATE PICTURES, MOODS, EMOTIONS

Everyone will admit poetry is a prime example of picture painting with words. But prose, to be moving, needs moving, descriptive words, too.

If you are trying to influence someone, your vocabulary can subconsciously reflect your mood or emotion. Bring this reflex to a level of consciousness.

Consider the soothing words: soft, serene, sleep, whisper. How about push, batter, clobber? In sound alone, they convey their meaning.

In sentences, verbs are the action words. Try to keep them clean and clear. How about this: "He walked softly" or, "He tiptoed"? The second is more descriptive. You can make up your own verb: "He slippered." This may be better.

Public relations men are well aware of the value of words to create pictures, to influence purchasing. In one experiment, two lots of the same stockings were placed on two separate sales tables. One merely gave the price. The other bore the title "Midnight Mist." Ten times as many of the named lot were sold.

Food creates a physical reaction. Describe luscious, steaming ears of corn dripping in butter, the fragrance of roast turkey mingled with the piquancy of sage dressing. Everyone will begin to swallow, to relive his past succulent dinners.

Doctors use this reaction for diagnostic purposes. Patients under the fluoroscope are asked to name their favorite foods. One young man described a rare steak smothered in

135

onions. His eyes narrowed as he "saw" it; his fingers measured the size; his nose wrinkled as he "sniffed" the remembered aroma. And his stomach? It went into action immediately.

If you have time to expand your thoughts, do more than state a fact. Suppose you want to describe an old farmhouse. Neil Morgan wrote this: " . . . a weathered, abandoned farmhouse, its roof collapsed, subsided into the landscape."

Can't you "see" that farmhouse? You, too, can find a different word to describe your scene so that your audience has a visual stimulation as well as an aural one.

TAKE A POSITIVE POSITION

Words filled with hope, words with a positive appeal, will be enjoyed, will have more impact than depressing, weakening words. If you can build your talk on an upswing, rather than dwelling on troubles, you are more apt to hold your audience.

We all realize that our minds try to bury unhappy events. Our days of joy and accomplishment overshadow those of doubt and despair.

So it is with a speech. Horror tales, direful warnings are effective for the moment, but words of optimism, showing the way to build a better future, will endure longer.

The words should be understandable and strong, attractive and meaningful.

Lenin was considered a poor speaker. He concentrated on slogans, using them over and over again. They were simple. They were positive. They had mass appeal. And what happened?

You may not wish to cause such a tremendous upheaval as the Russian Revolution or become the center of hero worship, but you can learn from his technique, how to influence those around you.

13 Influence Others Through Your Personality

A lot of things go into a speech to influence others—hard work with research, organization of ideas, a pleasing voice, appropriate vocabulary, meaningful gestures. But the most essential part of any speaker is his personality.

Gimmicks, creating a new vocabulary, using your hands in graceful or purposeful motions, are secondary to your personality.

Can you imagine Dean Martin trying to whip up enthusiasm to support a bird sanctuary? Eric Sevareid urging women to wear mini-skirts? George Wallace eulogizing Martin Luther King?

You probably are not typecast as they are, but your acquaintances have a fairly good idea of your interests and characteristics. Trying to speak in favor of an issue that does not appeal to you is like wearing clothes that belong to someone else with a different size.

How can you let your personality shine through and make your ideas powerful?

1. Let your emotions and opinions color your speech.
2. Concentrate your attention on your listeners, not yourself.
3. You are more important than your clothes.
4. Warmth and enthusiasm are more stimulating than perfection.
5. A sense of humor can be cultivated.
6. Let the "I," "me," and "my" be understood, not underlined.
7. Realize that you are important, your ideas are worthwhile, and you can influence others for their own good.

The *you* in your speech is the reason you are asked to speak. The *you* in your speech may be the catalyst that stimulates or influences your listeners.

YOUR EMOTIONS AND OPINIONS ADD COLOR TO YOUR IDEAS

How you feel about your subject is important. Let your emotions show. You will add color to your thoughts.

Most of the information you will be giving your listeners could find out for themselves. They want to know how *you* regard the situation, how *you* enjoyed your travel adventure, how *you* made a profit on the market when everyone else lost, how *you* overcame a problem.

There is a time for an impartial presentation, but even then, you do not have to be poker-faced. A smile is the same in any language. A warm approach does not imply any lack of dignity or respect. Be natural.

If you are a blunt individual, your opinion may be sought for just that reason. Oscar Levant, who seldom has a gracious word to say, once remarked, "The first thing I do in the morning is brush my teeth and sharpen my tongue."

Your personality is your own, unlike any other, emotionally charged by incidents that you may no longer remember, occasionally changed as you become more sensitive and knowledgeable.

If you don't like something for a justifiable reason, say so:

"People who toss beer cans along the road should be heavily fined."
"Super-highway planners who omit bicycle paths lack foresight."

Unless you are very sure of your facts and willing to face slander suits, avoid critical remarks about specific people or organizations. A terse complaint, clothed in witty words, however, may add spice to an otherwise slow-moving talk. After all, you are not expected to love everybody and everything. But use this gift of satire with restraint.

Anger is best directed at things or ways of behaving rather than individuals. Love, on the other hand, is constructive and laudatory, and names *should* be mentioned.

"Durwood English is a conscientious leader."
"Bob Thomas never fails to impress thoughtful citizens."
"The organizational abilities and leadership of Buck Engle are outstanding."

Take every opportunity to praise or appreciate publicly the people connected with your subject. After all, their well-deserved reputations may influence some dubious listeners.

CONCENTRATE ON YOUR LISTENERS

Just who are they out there listening to you? Are they with you? Are they looking at you critically, ready to pick you and your subject apart?

Generally, no. You will know ahead of time if you are to speak to a hostile audience. You must decide for yourself if your ideas are worth the aggravation that you know will come.

For the average speaker, the audience is on his side. But it must be met halfway. Your listeners are hoping to learn something or to be entertained. They want you to succeed.

Most people, particularly in the beginning, are nervous when they open their talk. William Jennings Bryan confessed to a weakness in the pit of his stomach. Cicero, one of the greatest orators of all time, shook visibly.

Cornelia Otis Skinner, who spent many years on the luncheon speakers' circuit, tells us that any time she becomes overawed or worried, she pictures her listeners sitting there in their underwear.

What essentially is shyness? Too great concern for your own self, worry or anxiety about how *you* appear to others. Forget yourself. Think about your audience, making them at ease, explaining your thoughts so clearly that *they* will understand. Replace fear with faith in yourself and thoughtfulness for others.

As Eleanor Roosevelt once remarked, "No one can make you feel inferior without your consent."

Your friends will be understanding; your enemies may not. Both have a pre-conceived opinion of you, and there is little you can do to change it. Do the best you can, and let it go at that. Comfort yourself with the fact that if your listeners could do better, they would be where you are.

If you don't want to be judged, you will say nothing, do nothing, and inevitably, you will *be* nothing. Stand up and be counted. Leaders are courageous. They accept criticism. But their influence, if their ideas are defensible and creative, grows.

YOU ARE MORE IMPORTANT THAN YOUR CLOTHES

Your clothes should become you. They should be so comfortable that you are unaware of them, but not so comfortable that they offend your audience. Always remember that they are the frame, but you are the picture.

If your clothes are more important than you, you're

either lecturing on fashion, proving a point, or not being intelligent.

Fashion commentators have to be extremely well-dressed, perhaps a step ahead of conventional fashion, but not so far out that their personalities are lost in contemplation of their appearance. One fashion show commentator, Midge Neff Mills, wears a bustle-backed gown of the mid-nineteenth century because she presides over historical fashion shows.

Herbert True, a lecturer on the professional circuit, occasionally wears a black-and-white striped "convict" uniform. His dress is meant to be startling.

Generally, however, the most important consideration should be cleanliness and good grooming. Unless you have been caught at the last moment and have no time to shave or dress appropriately, you have no excuse for a poor appearance.

If you are speaking at a dinner meeting, you should be aware of your face and teeth. Shelley Berman has an amusing comedy routine in which the hero builds up to a romantic high, only to be defeated by a small piece of spinach on his teeth. Certainly, a last-minute check of your appearance is not a matter of vanity. Rather, it is a sensible awareness that unimportant details can distract from your speech.

Untidiness and poor grooming, the kind usually associated with an absent-minded professor, are impolite. If you respect your audience and your subject, respect your appearance. Tuxedos may be the dress of the evening, but seldom so. Wear dark conventional suits for formal occasions or casual shirts with sports jackets, if your topic and the occasions lend themselves to that type of dress.

Ladies have to beware of too ornate or noisy jewelry, and their hats must frame their faces rather than hide them. Hair styles should be subdued to the point of not being more important than your features. Coiffeurs that are too radical will detract from your theme.

At one time, sophisticates wore dark glasses. When your listeners cannot see your eyes, you have lost an asset in any presentation. Be sure you have no barriers to easy communication.

WARMTH AND ENTHUSIASM ARE
MORE STIMULATING THAN PERFECTION

In a diamond, in a surgical operation, in a machine, perfection is essential or worth a greater price. But standards against which the product or performance can be measured are present.

In a speech, what is perfection? I once was asked to judge an extemporaneous speech contest in which the contestants were given the subject "Faith." There were five ladies, all beautifully groomed, intelligent, and well-practiced in the essentials of good speechmaking.

I have never had such a dull evening. They did nothing wrong. We could not put down minus points on the evaluation sheet. Their voices had variety; their speech was perfect and appropriate; they moved naturally, looked at their listeners, had a few anecdotes.

What was wrong? Perhaps the most obvious fault was that they were not "on fire" with their topic. And, too, they had carefully concealed all those endearing personality differences that make a person an individual. A computer could have made their points equally well.

Perfection is not what you seek. You want your listeners to understand, to appreciate, to act, to feel as you do, to be influenced.

CULTIVATE A SENSE OF HUMOR

Some people always see the funny side. Others predict gloom constantly. As speakers, they are nervous about themselves, their surroundings, their props. Relax, and take what happens in your stride.

When Bob Cockrell pushed his chair back too far and fell off the raised platform at the head table, everyone gasped.

When Bob came up smiling with a wave of reassurance, the speaker remarked, "I didn't realize my statement was so moving."

There's nothing like a big mistake for gaining anyone's attention. If you know you've made one, you have two recourses. Should you barge ahead, hoping that no one has noticed? That virtually never happens. There's always one who is aware. If the error is merely grammatical, stopping the thread of your discourse is foolish. If your argument will suffer because your tongue has become tangled and your statement has come out incorrectly, you'd better back up and start again.

If you can turn the mistake into a laugh at yourself, you have a golden opportunity. People can identify with speakers who are not perfect. The tension caused by a fluff is eased, and complete relaxation is all the more welcome. In fact, some professionals, having made a mistake and recovered it nicely, have been known to make the same mistake intentionally at later engagements. This takes a bit of doing and is not recommended for an amateur.

We can consider ourselves lucky that we are not as concerned as the Japanese about "losing face." A college professor told our class of an experience he had while teaching a class of Japanese students. One member of the class, leaning back in his chair during the lecture, fell backwards and was very embarrassed. Before the class was over, all the students had fallen over, too, to "save face" for him.

Robert L. Ripley tells of an experience he had, giving a talk before an Eastern prep school. He was extremely flattered by the almost devout attention on the part of the young boys. A few even took notes.

After the event, he questioned one of the more assiduous scribblers, asking what interested him so much that he wanted to write it down.

"Oh sir," was the reply, "our English master gives us extra credits for catching mistakes that lecturers make when they talk. I just can't remember all of them for class the next day."

Ripley discovered that his mistakes had totalled a new high that semester!

BE SUBTLE

While we are stressing the fact that it is you and your personality that make the difference in almost any subject, the "you" in your talk has to be subtle.

Too much "I," "me," and "my" scattered throughout any speech acts like a heavy screen. It diffuses a clear picture of the subject, keeping the listener at a distance. Long ago, editors discovered that "we" is a preferable pronoun if a pronoun is to be used.

If you are discussing a country, focus on the country. Your reactions to it should be individual and different without continually pounding on the fact that *you* took the trip. Your description of the people and places will be personal, chosen because of your particular interests—as they should be!

In reviewing books or supporting a campaign, indicate your opinions without slamming them home as personal. Use yourself if you must, occasionally, to indicate that you can goof. If you are explaining a process or routine at work for new employees, you can insert your own experiences only if they are used not to flatter yourself. You know the difference.

Continually tell people how good you are, how efficient you are, and unconsciously, they will look for the flaws. Be modest—not falsely so—and they will appreciate and notice your abilities.

Australian psychologist Paul R. Wilson made a study of the ways people formed their impressions of others.

He asked separate groups of students to estimate a man's height. Introduced as just another student, the man was judged to be just under 5'10" by the first group. The second group, who were told he was a lecturer, thought he was over 5'10". The third group shot him up to almost 6' when he was introduced as a senior lecturer. As a professor from Cambridge, he was judged by the last group as over 6'. This test was run only on appearance.

The impression you make on your listeners will grow if you give them something to enjoy or further their knowledge. Give them of yourself. They want that. They don't want egotists, however, using them as a mirror for self-adulation.

RECOGNIZE YOUR OWN WORTH

You can do anything you really want to do; you can be as influential as you want to be.

The secret is to believe in yourself, to see yourself in the role you desire—and work toward that goal.

There are volumes upon volumes of information to help you discover your potential. If you want to explore the subject, we can recommend two books on the subject:

- Goeller, Carl J. and William O. Uraneck, *13 Steps to a Dynamic Personality*. Parker Publishing Company, Inc., 1971. 224 pp.
- Fowler, Jack. *Patterns of Success*. Parker Publishing Company, Inc., 1972. 224 pp.

Your estimate of yourself is evident to your listeners. Let them follow a man who believes in his ideas, believes in them so much he wants to share them, to influence others to enjoy a better tomorrow.

14

Humor Can Influence an Audience to Listen

PEOPLE want to be entertained far more than they want to be taught. Spice your talks with humor. If you can incorporate both information and wit in one speech, you will have listeners. And as we have said before, only people who listen can be influenced.

Man is the only animal who can laugh. Sometimes his laughter is directed at things, sometimes at people. A few laugh at the troubles of others. Most of us laugh at ourselves when a difficult situation has retreated far enough back into time to be no longer painful.

Humor can be classified into many different styles. You will have to choose yours. What will it be?

1. Pungent, one-sentence quips—dry wit.
   a. Unexpected twists
   b. Satire
   c. Puns
2. Exaggeration—folk-type humor.
   a. Tall tales
   b. Understatement
   c. Confusion
3. Anecdotes—whimsy.
4. Parodies, limericks.
5. Movement alone.

A few people have a natural gift. Most work hard to cultivate finesse. Win Pendleton, one of America's most capable humorists, says he practices constantly to keep his stories sharp, uncluttered with extra words, his intonation correct, his pacing exactly right, and the punchline precise.

Try out your stories on your friends and family. If they don't laugh, your audience won't either. Listen to yourself on a tape recorder. Would you be amused? A funny story that falls flat is worse than no attempt at all. Your audience is embarrassed for you, and your dignity is diminished.

HUMOR HAS MANY USES

There are at least five reasons for adding humor to an otherwise serious dissertation:

1. As transition to the main subject.
2. To develop rapport with the audience.
3. To relieve tension.
4. To make a point.
5. In emergencies, to reclaim the attention of the audience.

You may not need humor to cover all these points. You may not, in fact, have enough time to use humor to a large extent.

We have all heard speakers begin with a story, often only slightly tied in with their subjects. Many, and this includes professionals, make no effort to associate topic and tale. One declares this is his way of measuring his range. He has, from past experience, discovered which stories are certain to evoke laughter. If the man up in the balcony is not moved, the speaker knows he isn't being heard.

Perhaps the best reason to begin a talk with a humorous incident is that laughter establishes a quick rapport with the audience. Some speakers feel that listeners are not always ready to listen immediately to serious ideas. They need a settling-down period, and the short anecdote gives them the opportunity, because the average story does not require too much concentration to be understood.

Generally speaking, the main reason to use a funny story is to make a point. If, afterwards, only the story is remembered, you have failed. One geometry teacher was so anxious to impress upon his pupils' minds the position of a right angle, that he stood on his head to illustrate the relationship.

Years later, one of his students met him on the street, grasped his hand warmly, then remarked, "I'll never forget you—the way you stood on your head in class! By the way, why did you do that?"

In your use of humor, don't go overboard. Laughs have their place, but too many will bury the seriousness of your main ideas.

Laughter gives everyone a chance to relax. Amusing stories give your audience a breathing space, a chance to absorb what has just been said. However, be relevant. Dragging in a story to make a definite break between your arguments may be relaxing, but if you lose the thread of your talk, you may confuse some of your listeners.

Audiences will laugh or move in response to humor, and the physical activity alone will keep them alert and ready to hear what you are saying. Puns are considered the lowest form of humor, and the expected response is always a groan. Look at it realistically. Isn't this audience participation? Movement and noise stimulate people, reawaken their interest.

Mistakes or mishaps can always occur when you are in front of a group. Lead the laughter. Turn the trouble into a joke against yourself if you can.

Brighten every talk with wit or humor. As Logan Pearsall Smith once said, "Humorous quotations are the salted almonds at reason's feast."

SHORT QUIPS EVOKE INTEREST

If your group is intellectual, you can use a higher level of material. One-line quips or unexpected phrases are over too soon for some listeners. Like Jack Benny, you can pause and wait for the audience, but if the point is at all obscure, your wait may be futile.

Quips are witticisms in which the general statement is made, followed by an unexpected twist. Here are a few:

A bird in the hand is—messy.

Of course, women aren't what they used to be—they used to be girls.

A friend in need is—a pest.

Do unto others—then, cut out in a hurry.

The pause is essential, and a pause just before the quip sets it off as well; otherwise, the whole sentence may be lost.

Satire, also a more intellectual form of humor, is extremely difficult to use without resorting to a heavy-handed attack. It often gives offense, and unless your audience is objective, they may not be able to accept or understand the point you are trying to make. Here's an old favorite:

What a lovely dress you have on! Too bad they didn't have one in your size.

Despite the groans, most people thoroughly enjoy puns. They often take time to be understood. Be sure your listeners have this time. A pause before you begin and after you end is, again, important. Here are several:

> *The more perfect a man is, the more girls try to altar him.*
>
> *Buy our bread, we knead the dough.*
>
> *Better to have loved a short girl than never to have loved at all.*

Oscar Wilde said a long time ago, "Puns are the lowest form of humor when you don't think of it first."

OBVIOUS EXAGGERATION DELIGHTS MOST LISTENERS

If you have more time or a less sophisticated audience, you can rely upon out-of-balance remarks—exaggerated or understated.

Texans have long been noted for their tall tales. Children love them, and most adults have enough of the child in them to appreciate absurdities. Here's two samples:

> *The heat was so terrific last week that I saw a hound dog chasing a rabbit; they were both walking.*
>
> *My team is the only one that can play a double-header and lose three games.*

Distort your ideas until they are ridiculous and so, laughable. All should draw attention to the specific thought you are trying to emphasize.

Go to the other extreme. Nothing is funnier than a dramatic understatement:

> *If at first you don't succeed, well, so much for sky-diving.*
>
> *Oscar Levant once said, "My wife divorced me last week on the grounds of incompatibility, and, besides I think she hated me."*

For raising simple ideas to conspicuous idiocy, you can fall back on what is called "governmentese." Directions to perform any task or ordinary explanations are given in such a torrent of words that the listener or reader is often lost:

> *Due to a metabolic inability to cope with a recent change, I did not respond to external stimuli, thereby remaining in a comatose condition. (The alarm clock failed to waken me when my work hours were changed.)*

Norm Crosby has made a reputation for himself by telling serious stories but using big words that are incorrect. This is called "malapropism."

For example: *Women thrive on love and affliction, but men tend to put them on a pinochle.*

These obvious distortions delight listeners, but use them sparingly as highlights—unless, of course, your main purpose is to amuse.

ANECDOTES ARE FOR EVERYONE

A story must be properly told to make a point. It must be carefully told if it is to be amusing. But the whole world enjoys a tale.

There are five essentials in telling a funny story.

1. Know the story thoroughly.
2. Keep it short for a sharper point.
3. Speak distinctly.
4. Set off your punchline.
5. Laugh only after your audience begins to laugh.

Be sure that you can remember your story clear through to the punchline before you start. Tell it with sincerity, without an introduction. "That reminds me of a story . . ." is unimaginative and unnecessary. Jump right into your tale, as though it really had happened. Maybe it did; maybe it's a tale that is particularly appropriate. If you want to be honest about its artificiality, wait until afterwards. You can say then, "Well, that's the way I heard it" or, "It could have happened that way."

Chances are, most people will expect that the stories are fiction. They don't really care, nor are they too analytical if they can enjoy a laugh. If you can, personalize the story. Make it sound as though it happened to you—or could have.

Keep your story short. The more astute listeners will try to beat you to the punchline anyway. Maybe they've heard the story before, or maybe they're just guessing. Don't give them time. Get to the finish with no extra words thrown in.

Above all, speak distinctly. One simple word often makes all the difference in understanding a story. Slow down your speech if you notice your audience is straining. Unless you are intentionally deadpanning, be dramatic. Move around. Act out the parts that you can. Enjoy yourself as you do.

The punchline or ending must come with a sharpness, a distinctness that causes it to stand out and makes it completely clear to all the listeners. Slow down your story as you approach the punchline. Pause for a second. Then, deliver it.

Wait for your audience to laugh. You may have failed so dismally to put your point across that no one gets it, and, therefore, no one laughs. Laughing alone up on a platform is a disaster. If the joke fails, leave it. Any explanation is less than desirable. Go on to your next point.

If, however, all has gone well, and the audience is laughing, let them enjoy the moment. You can be amused with them before you proceed to the next assertion.

PARODIES AND PERSONAL LIMERICKS PLEASE

Enterprising speakers can use familiar poems, either giving them a reverse twist and making them very short or utilizing long stories. They take a bit longer to work out if you want to be original, but they are delightful and much appreciated.

Hickory dickory dock
Two mice ran up the clock

The clock struck one;
The other got away.

Mary had a little lamb.
Was the doctor surprised!

Or use Rudyard Kipling's "If":

If you can keep your head when all about you are losing
theirs—you haven't got all the facts.

" 'Twas the Night Before Christmas" has inspired many
to develop their own themes:

Merry Christmas, amigos.
'Twas the night before Christmas, and all through the
casa
Not a creature was stirring—caramba, que pasa? ......
. . . .
or,

'Twas the day before payday, and all round the place
The fellows were borrowing, for it's no disgrace
To run short of money, one day too soon.
Our checks don't come round till Friday at noon . . .

The idea is old, but the ambitious speaker's adaptation
is new and enjoyable. If you're clever, you can make a point in
your doggerel.

Limericks are fun, too. They can be found in many
collections. One of my favorites is:

Said an envious, erudite, ermine
There's one thing I cannot determine
   When a dame wears my coat
   She's a person of note.
When I wear it, I'm only a vermin.

With a small amount of effort and ingenuity, you can
write your own.

There once was a fellow called Russ,

A Toastmaster we'd like to discuss
He's president now
A true-blue highbrow
With ideas that sure stimulate us.

The poetry may not be so earthshaking, but the limerick is personalized and, therefore, much more attention-getting.

MOVEMENT ADDS MERRIMENT

If you are naturally an outgoing person, you can use your body to add humor to a situation, tossing your head, winking broadly, shrugging.

Flip Wilson has an engaging hip-wiggle and finger-snapping motion that is almost a trademark. But, you probably won't require that much exaggeration unless, again, your stress is on entertainment alone.

Don't forget, too—if movement is embarrassing for you, lack of movement is also effective. A poker-face has put over many a joke.

GOOD JOKES ARE LIKE GOOD MUSIC

No one complains when concert pianists present the same music again and again. No one remarks, "I've heard that before." Surprisingly, most listeners are willing to laugh at old jokes, particularly if they're dressed up to meet the moment.

A New Yorker, who collects jokes as a hobby, has more than 3 million in his collection. Many of them, he says, are merely switches or updating of old material. He bewails the fact that comedians never surprise him anymore.

Luckily for us, we won't be speaking often before such professionals. Listen to any of the celebrated television comics. Watch yourself objectively. You laugh, don't you? And haven't you heard or seen most of their routines before?

Perhaps the only important consideration is to choose material that has not just been published in the local paper, or the *Reader's Digest,* or the "chuckle section" of the journal of the organization to which your audience belongs.

Jokes run in waves. When General MacArthur delivered his mournful line, "Old soldiers never die; they just fade away," jokesters went off on a delirious tangent.

> *Old fishermen never die; they just smell that way.*
> *Old tourists never die; they just lose their grip.*
> *Old pickpockets never die; they just steal away.*

You can make up your own, depending upon the group you are addressing.

Then, there was the era of the "slim book" led off by: The slimmest book to appear on the market is General DeGaulle's *How to Win Friends.* You can create some of your own. How about *How to Win a War* by General Custer? All of these are "old," but the way you use them is new if you apply a personal twist or relationship.

A playwright named Terence, who was born in 190 B.C., deplored, "Nothing is said nowadays that has not been said before."

If people have been repeating things for more than 2,000 years, who are you to be different? Tell the oldies. Polish them up, and aim them at the right individuals. They will enjoy them. And you may be lucky, they may not have heard all the stories you have.

NEVER, NEVER, NEVER

There are a few basic don'ts that should be remembered. Most of them are so elementary that everyone recognizes them although they may not always observe them. A few we have touched on earlier in this chapter or elsewhere.

Avoid trite introductions, such as "That reminds me . . ." or "A funny thing happened to me on the way . . ." Equally, avoid trite transitions as you continue, "Seriously though . . ." or, "But to get back to important things . . ."

Don't telegraph your punchline. Let your finish be a

surprise, an unexpected twist or remark. Try this: *Behind every successful man is* (pause) *a surprised mother-in-law.* These are matters of technique which can be accomplished by practice.

What is most important, however, is your choice of material. No matter how funny a situation or story is, if it offends anyone, it should be omitted. Leave it out! Risqué stories are risky. The barriers are going down swiftly on the public platform, over television and radio, but this is one time when leadership is a doubtful distinction.

Beyond risqué humor, derogatory humor is also questionable. Will Rogers said he made fun only of those "big enough" to take it. Is anyone "big enough"? He may laugh with the crowd but some of the remarks may stick and hurt. In the end, this type of humor reflects against the person who is funny at another person's expense.

There are well-known comedians who thrive on imaginary flamboyant feuds, but generally speaking, the humor is so absurd that it will not be believed. Most comedians using derogatory humor have short-lived popularity. If you must poke fun at someone, let it be yourself. The audience will enjoy that, and with the contrariness of man, will not believe a word you say against yourself. Unless you overdo this self-criticism to the point of boredom, you will be remembered as modest and humorous.

Whatever you choose to do, do it with confidence. Occasionally, novice speakers feel apologetic about inserting a light note. They drop their voices, fumble their punchlines, or try to read the material. If this happens to you, you need more practice before a mirror, or with a tape recorder, or both.

Remember, the ability to understand and appreciate humor is a sign of normalcy. Fanatics or mentally disturbed people cannot turn aside from their burning, dogmatic ideas.

RESEARCH FOR FUN

Clipping stories from magazines and papers, making sure

to date them, as well as note the source, will provide an invaluable reservoir of material.

There are jokebooks in stores and at newsstands, and your library, too, is sure to have a selection. Look for these titles:

- William R. Gerler. *Executive's Treasury of Humor for Every Occasion.* New York, Parker Publishing Co., Inc., 1965. 256 pp.
- Herbert Prochnow. *A Dictionary of Wit, Wisdom, and Satire.* New York, Harper and Row, 1962. 285 pp.
- Bennett Cerf. *The Life of the Party.* Garden City, N. Y., Doubleday, 1956. 247 pp.

Material is arranged according to subject or author and is easy to locate and use.

Choose what is relevant, stories so old that they are fresh, or ones that can be adapted to present events. Add your own touch, personalizing incidents.

This is one time when research is really fun. Chuckle while you choose. And when you have chosen, charm your audience into following your proposals.

15 Questions Can Lead to Influencing Statements

SOCRATES came to a bad end because he asked too many questions, they say. Still, he amassed a tremendous amount of knowledge for himself and led others into new thought channels by questioning them, before he was summarily removed from this life in his seventieth year.

No one grows intellectually without questioning, silently of himself or vocally of others. When someone is too ignorant about any subject, the common remark is, *"I'm too stupid even to know what to ask."* Most advances in knowledge come from an unsatisfied wonderer or dreamer who poses the question *"why?"* or *"what if . . .?"*

Questions fall into two categories in the average speech: those you ask the audience and those they ask you. Questions with answers in the body of a speech are excellent ways to organize information. There, you have time to reveal answers you have already discovered. When you throw open any meeting to answer queries from your listeners, you are taking a chance. Do you know enough? Are you self-confident enough to think on your feet? Can you admit ignorance without feeling embarrassed?

Questions a speaker uses fall into two categories:

1. For information, requiring audience response.
2. Rhetorical questions that:
   a. Lead into a new idea and are, therefore, transitional.
   b. Stimulate thinking during the discussion.
   c. Challenge—those that finish off the talk.

Questions from your audience can be categorized:

1. Those that want clarification.
2. Those that want more information.
3. Those that show dissension.
4. Those that are agreeing, used to show off the questioner.
5. Those that are foolish.

ANSWER YOUR OWN QUESTIONS FIRST

You can open your talk with a question. You can introduce your ideas in question form, then proceed to explain them fully. You can close your talk with a question.

There are all sorts of questions, but with all forms your voice changes, arresting attention. Your listeners are alerted to a new line you are planning to follow. They put themselves in the place of the questioner. You establish rapport quickly.

Informational questions are great devices to gain attention. Remember the enthusiastic response given when a speaker asks where his listeners come from?

How many Brooklynites are here?
Anyone from California?

Handkerchiefs wave; whistles pierce the ears. These questions establish rapport and allow the audience to participate.

Some questions about the audience's experiences help the speaker to establish his foundation. If no one has ever seen a hockey game, he can find out:

How many of you have seen an ice hockey game?

or, on another subject:

Have any of you read Guy Shackley's instructions for field procedure?

Audiences are delighted to respond, and the speaker is able to adjust his preliminary remarks to meet their needs.

Rhetorical questions are not posed to be answered out loud. Listeners recognize them as such. Some may nod or smile, but usually that will be the extent of their response.

When hecklers are present, however, the speaker had better forego asking any questions and use only affirmative statements. The pause after a question, that allows sympathetic listeners to think, may be a welcome opening for a dissenter to shout his opposition.

Leading questions are popular to open a talk or to introduce a new argument.

Did you realize that there are 7,500 foreclosures a month in our state?

This sentence is taken directly from the opening of a talk to support a new property tax law. As the speaker continued, he used questions at every new thought.

Do you know that property owners pay almost 4% of the assessed value of their homes?
What will the new bill do for us?

The first question conveys information. The second is used as a lead-in to presenting information.

Often questions are used to stimulate thinking:

What would result if we hired three more people to work with young drug addicts?

What programs can we suggest to Hap Owens to bring in more members?

160

In this case, you are not planning to give definitive answers. The answers are not yet discovered. The audience can use its own creative imagination.

End with a question. The question may be a direct challenge:

> *What are you going to do about protecting our young adults from drug pushers?*
>
> *Are you going to be one of the enlightened voters who supports John Dower in his candidacy?*

Questions, properly used, do much to stimulate thinking about your subject, to keep audiences alert, to help the speaker develop vocal variety. Use them to influence your listeners to think, hopefully to follow your ideas and proposals.

QUESTIONS FROM THE AUDIENCE

Are you sure there will be questions? Nothing is more embarrassing than to say brightly, "Now, if there are any questions, I'll be glad to answer them," and have the audience sit mutely, shifting in their seats.

If you have prepared well, and your audience is alert, you will have stimulated interest. You should have questions waiting for you. Occasionally, however, audiences are reluctant to begin. Avoid this situation; plant a question or two with friends in the audience. They need not be asked if other questions come immediately. If only those two questions are asked, you will know that you've either covered your subject very well, or no one cares to know any more.

Discover before you offer to answer questions if this is convenient. Make arrangements ahead of time with the organization that is sponsoring your talk. Time or your position on the program may be factors that will influence their decision.

With the best will in the world, you cannot answer every question that may arise. Physically, the group may be too large. There may be too many in number, or the acoustics not good enough In this event, explain beforehand that you either are willing to answer questions for a specific length of time or that you cannot answer oral questions at all.

For large groups, request that questions be written on slips of paper that can be collected following your talk. Have ushers ready with paper to distribute. Having questions written will solve many problems that could arise. Sometimes, written questions are screened by assistants to avoid repetition or frivolous queries. Priority should be given to questions of most general interest.

Why do people ask questions? Some people want to know more, probably about one special point. Can you expand on that? Others aren't sure what you meant. Perhaps your vocabulary confused them. They haven't encountered the basic ideas before and need to have you go over somethi g, using different words or images that will clarify your point. Still others want to know why *you* feel the way you do. Are you justified in interpreting the facts that way?

Answers to these questions should be easy. They are direct and meaningful. Unfortunately, all your questions may not be.

You have held the floor for a time. Jealousy stirs in the hearts of some of your listeners. They will rise to a question, but within a few words, it is obvious that all they want is attention. They may be rephrasing your talk or voicing judgment on your remarks. Perhaps, they just want their opinion to be heard. The sentences may be formed as questions, but you have only to nod in agreement and accept their remarks, or try to stem their flow of oratory. If you accept only written questions, these people will be restrained.

Some attention-seekers are completely opposed to your point of view and want to be sure to enlighten the audience before it disperses. Their questions are seldom gentle. They may be vicious, or phrased so that either you have to repeat what you have already said or refuse to be led off on a tangent. A dignified disagreement is the best response. Most of the listeners will be with you.

Do not indulge in debate. Cut off your dissenter as politely as you can. Tell him he has a point well-taken if you think so. Thank him, but say firmly that you have not found evidence to support his claims.

And then, there are the foolish who betray themselves and unconsciously reveal their inadequacy. Do not go over the entire speech for them. Make a simple point, then suggest that they can read about the subject if they desire to know more about it. Whatever you do, don't show arrogance or impatience with them.

You may, occasionally, get flip questions that you can turn into a laugh.

Carol Channing was once asked, "Do you remember the most embarrassing moment of your life?"

"Yes, I certainly do," she said. "Next question?"

WHAT HAVE YOU GOT TO SAY TO THAT?

There's a proper way to answer questions. Teachers are warned in pedagogy classes never to repeat questions. In a large hall without microphones for the listeners, questions should be restated.

Repeat them in slightly different words. Why? First of all, you want to be sure everyone hears what has been asked. Secondly, by varying the words, you are making sure you know not only the exact request but also that you have interpreted it correctly. This checks on both your hearing and your comprehension. Sometimes the questioner does not realize the ambiguity of his words until he hears them funneled through another mind.

Having ascertained that you are truly communicating, answer the question. You have had some time to formulate your thoughts while you were going through this procedure. Your subconscious has been given the opportunity to whip through your vast storehouse of accumulated knowledge.

Recognize your questioners insofar as you can, according

163

to the order in which they have risen or raised their hands. If someone wants to ask a second question, give priority to those who are attempting to ask their first question. Vary, if possible, your attention from one side of the room to the other.

Be concise in your replies. Dan Tyler Moore, a popular speaker, reserves his statistics for this period, feeling that they give weight to his remarks but are not colorful enough to include in the main talk.

You will hear a few unanswerable questions. Maybe you lack the knowledge; maybe the answer has not yet been determined. Don't apologize; don't guess; don't hedge. You are not expected to be a walking encyclopedia. If you guess wrong, you can be sure most of your listeners will not only find out but will remember you for that mistake as well. One misquote or error will undermine almost all you have said before.

Evasiveness is a poor reaction. Admit you don't know the answer. If you have an explanation, give it. Is the requested information really in your field? You may not have had time or the desire to investigate in that direction. If it relates to material for which there is no known answer, say so.

Some questions are so broad that you cannot begin to answer. A whole new field, another long speech, would have to be given. Thank the questioner for his interest, but decline. Explain that you do not have the time to do justice to the subject. Steer him onto books that may be helpful, if you know of any.

Here are three warnings! Do not carry on a conversation or debate with your questioner. No matter how interesting it may be to you, this is not the time to explore some other tangent. If the question seems ridiculous, avoid the temptation to make a witty remark that is face-losing for your questioner. And lastly, keep your temper, no matter how discourteous a questioner may seem.

Socrates spent a lifetime questioning. You can develop your skill to build success in public speaking. You can ask questions that will influence your listeners to think.

16

The Extras that Build Influence into a Speech

BY this point, you know all the fundamentals that go into developing a top-notch talk; informative, persuasive, narrative, or humorous. How you use the suggestions will depend upon your point of view—your frame of reference plus your personality.

Every situation, every speech has a different dimension or a different framework to set it off.

Few speakers begin their speech the moment they reach the lectern. There are traditional acknowledgments.

While we have covered the essentials in the past few chapters, there are other considerations.

With these in mind, we plan to devote this chapter to:

1. Before you begin your talk.
2. Poetry for enrichment.
3. Visual aids for clarification.
4. Hazards of listening.

While these ideas are not essential, awareness of them can start off your talk properly, make it more fluent or more understandable, and stimulate more listeners. What does that add up to? More influence.

BEFORE THE TALK BEGINS

Most speakers have to make two beginnings. And both are important. Neither should be treated as inconsequential. One establishes rapport with the audience; the other should quicken interest in the subject. Unless you are well-acquainted with the group, establishing rapport depends upon a last-minute judgment. Even then, much of what you say will be tempered by your introduction.

There have been classic cases in which persons introducing the speaker have been so hungry for attention that they have infringed upon the speaking time. William Jennings Bryan lost his entire allocated time on two occasions.

Another time, a chairman took one hour to introduce the President of the United States at a national political convention. He had lost sight of the purpose of an introduction. Introductions are to make known the speaker, give his authority for speaking, and relate his subject to the group.

The information about you as the speaker should be accurate. You will be wise to enumerate clearly the important facts in your background, particularly as they relate to the group you are addressing.

If you are talking to the Sons of Italy and your name is Higgins, make sure they know your mother was from Naples and that you've lately visited Rome and Rapallo.

Your educational background, your vocational experiences, occasionally family facts, books or articles you may have authored—all of these will be important at different times before different groups.

Give them to the one who is to introduce you as early as you can, and also include the exact title of your talk. Write them down to be sure.

Even then, he may fluff. Clare Boothe Luce, who wrote the startling, witty play *The Women,* was once introduced as the author of "that immortal classic, *Little Women.*" Occasionally, your subject may be misinterpreted, given a different slant than you intended.

What can you do? You have a split-second decision to make. Correct the chairman and make him look foolish? Proceed and hope that your audience recognizes the error? Graciousness and tact are certainly required. Humor, using yourself as a target, if possible, may turn a difficult situation into an asset.

In some cases, you will be overpraised to the extent of feeling foolish. President Kennedy handled this nicely when he remarked with a smile, "With an introduction like that, I really should sit down right now while I'm ahead."

But, good or bad, you have been introduced. You are on your feet. The hush of expectancy fills the room. Where do you begin?

DON'T RECOGNIZE EVERYONE

You must, of course, acknowledge your introducer. Be complimentary, if you can, without being effusive or false.

Philip, the Duke of Edinburgh, has remarked, "It is my invariable custom to say something flattering to begin with, so that I shall be excused if by any chance I put my foot in it later on."

Ordinarily, a sweeping, comprehensive "Ladies and

Gentlemen" will do. If important people are present—town officials, national officers at a local meeting—they should be recognized, but only, however, if they are few in number.

If half a dozen assorted officials are present, it is better if you omit individual names. It is infinitely more devastating to forget one person than to lump all of them into one general group.

Besides, while the man mentioned may have his vanity assuaged, the rest of the audience is not too interested.

Recognize the group or the locality with a remark that is personal, if possible, that will appeal to their pride or emotions. This is the time to let your listeners know you appreciate them as individuals, that your purpose is to be helpful or informative. You are establishing empathy.

Hopefully, the microphone has been tested and is set at the correct spot. Don't move it unless you are sure it is not. Once, I took one apart and brought it forward from the end of the lectern, only to discover that it had been carefully adjusted for that exact distance. It took several minutes to readjust.

If you are not sure you can be heard, ask the audience. Once you have ascertained the correct range of your voice, you are ready.

APOLOGIZE—NEVER!

Skilled speakers know better than to apologize.

"I didn't have time to prepare." "I didn't know exactly what you wanted to hear." "I don't know why I was asked." "I'm sure some of you know more than I do about some aspects of the case." You've heard all these before. They have, unfortunately, been true too often.

Nothing irritates me more than the first remark. My time is valuable to me. No speaker has the right to stand up and tell me he could not find the time to prepare. Particularly, if the talk, you know, has been scheduled for a while. Sometimes the speaker is preparing his way for failure, giving his excuses beforehand.

Don't let that happen to you! Of course, there may be better-informed people listening to you. But they can't always communicate. You can! Someone has faith in you. Someone expects you to deliver. You will lower his reputation as well as your own if you sow seeds of doubt in your opening sentence.

Maybe you are a last-minute replacement for someone with a deservedly high reputation. That just makes it more of a challenge.

Give your audience your best. They will, very quickly, accept your judgment of yourself, particularly if it is self-debasing. And first impressions are apt to stick.

Give yourself the benefit of the doubt. Respect your own abilities without being arrogant. You are going to influence them to do or act as you suggest.

The preliminaries are over. You are ready to begin.

POETRY ENRICHES

Most people respond to poetry, whether it is a sonnet or mere doggerel. If you have a favorite line or two that seems particularly apt, include it.

You can begin or end your talk with poetry. Inserted into the body of a talk, it often provides a refreshing change of pace. If the lines are familiar, your listeners will smile with remembrance. If not, they will have to listen more assiduously.

Only three considerations should be made:

1. Choose relevant lines.
2. Pause before beginning.
3. Speak from memory, if possible.

With the wealth of poetry in collections, there is no lack of material to be used.

A talk on the weakness of man-made construction could be enhanced with Shelley's "Ozymandias."

Lewis Carroll's "Father William" could enliven a talk on old age. Quatrains from the *Rubáiyát* by Omar Khayyám are always effective in a philosophical discussion. Reach into the recesses of your memory for those lines that you enjoyed.

Whatever you do, pause before reciting poetry. The change of vocabulary and, occasionally, the grammar, is disconcerting to a listener who is not cued in.

Do not, however, stop abruptly and announce, "I am now going to recite . . ." Your audience will understand without being told

If you can, memorize the lines. They have more impact when you can look at your audience, not your notes. Do, however, keep a copy nearby. It is better to refer to a discreet little card than to flub a line.

VISUAL AIDS CLARIFY IDEAS

A speech before an audience is as much a visual performance as an audible one. They will be using their eyes constantly, probably with even more intensity than their ears.

Give them something to look at. We have already mentioned that action on your part keeps them awake.

Visuals generally include:

1. The object itself.
2. A model.
3. Pictures.
   a. Slides
   b. Movies
   c. Drawings
4. Maps and diagrams.

If you are discussing something that can be easily carried, show the object itself. A book reviewer should have a copy of the book. A promoter of Teflon cookware should display a sample product. Social workers describing drug problems generally carry marijuana roach clips and heroin kits. These articles give a third dimension to any lecture.

There are times, however, when the material is immovable or unwieldy. In this situation, models are often available. Your local government has prototypes of its major projects, such as bridges, community centers, and highway interchanges. Medical associations have models of various physical organs, diseased or healthy. Occasionally, museums will lend copies of artifacts or mock-ups. Schools, too, have many unusual models made by students in their projects. Look around before you decide that you have to make a model for yourself or do without.

Slides, carefully selected, with accurate colors and a pinpoint focus, are invaluable. But don't go overboard. Too many slides or too long an interval spent on individual views tires your viewers' eyes. When their eyes shut involuntarily, their minds tend to shut off as well.

Flash them on the screen. Make your point quickly. Go on to the next. When the Reverend Melvin Harter puts on a slide show for his friends and parishioners, he never loses anyone's attention. If their eyes aren't glued to the screen, they miss out, so short is the time he allows. And, of course, the pictures are all well worth seeing because he has omitted all those of minor interest.

Movies are harder to handle. If you can take and edit your own, you will have exactly what you want to show. Unfortunately, most of us have to use films provided by others. Be sure you see the film itself before foisting it on others. If it is not relevant or worthwhile, scrap it. Don't let your reputation as a speaker suffer from material that will not enhance your talk.

There are so many worthwhile sources of films, that a little scouting around will provide you with a varied selection. Many libraries have film bureaus. Travel agencies, chambers of commerce, universities, museums, and private corporations, such as *Time-Life,* have prepared material that is excellent and can be adapted to your talk.

How much more interesting is a talk on water contamination accompanied by an eight-minute film such as "Water:

Friend or Enemy?" This, available in the Cleveland Public Library, illustrates correct measures for keeping spring water clean.

Drawings are fun, if you have the ability to do them either before you come or on a board as you talk.

Maps and diagrams are excellent to illustrate relationships or locations.

Almost any visual aid can be an attention-arouser or interest-holder. It will make your subject clear and can save a proportionate number of words or lengthy explanations. It builds support for your ideas, which influences listeners.

LISTENING NEEDS UNDERSTANDING

Do you realize that under ordinary circumstances only 25% of your material will be retained by your listeners after 48 hours?

As a speaker, you must realize a few facts about the art of listening.

1. Listening requires effort.
2. Speakers use about 100 to 125 words a minute. Listeners think at a rate of up to 800 words a minute; therefore, the average listener concentrates only ten seconds out of every minute.
3. Listeners have prejudicial barriers against certain words.
4. The impression you make on them as you enter will affect their acceptance of your ideas.

Because you, as a speaker, are aware of these points, you will be prepared. When a listener has to work too hard to understand, he often turns off.

You will realize that the mind of every listener wanders. As speakers, we must not contribute to this on-off habit. We must concentrate on our topic, shun tangential thoughts that can weaken our main argument and give our listeners an excuse to drift.

We have already discussed the effect of words and

appearance on our listeners. Let us always think of our talks objectively from the listener's standpoint.

THE FINISHED SPEECH

Let us forget the platitudes. Forget the obvious, the dull, the oft-repeated, self-evident information. Let us stimulate our listeners with new ideas, creatively expressed. Remember, every time we speak, our minds are showing.

Let us develop our talks carefully, following the plan:

L atch on
E xplain
A mplify
D ramatize
S ummarize

Let us polish them, then add imaginative, clarifying, enjoyable touches.

Even then, you will find every speech you give includes four speeches: the speech as you plan to present it; the speech you do present; the speech your audience heard; and the speech you would give if you had to do it again.

You will, however, influence your listeners.

Section V

SPEECH SITUATIONS

17

You Can Influence People You Cannot See

DISEMBODIED voices can project warmth, doubt, anger, viciousness. We all recognize many people from their voices alone. When well-known actors portray cartoon characters, we often visualize the actor instead of the character. Does your voice always fit your moods? More important, can you dissemble so that you do not betray an emotion you don't want to reveal?

We all become involved in sightless communication when we use a telephone. Unlike radio or taping, there is, at least, interaction between the speakers. Reactions are immediate and oral. You can change your approach, adjust your tone, explain away misunderstandings.

Most of us accept tape recorders and telephones as

extensions of daily conversation, but a few thoughts about these electronic marvels can make our use of them more meaningful.

TELEPHONES REACH EVERYWHERE

Telephones have made it possible for us to extend our influence far beyond our physical boundaries. Our discoveries and our conclusions can be relayed for thousands of miles and affect industry. Our opinions and suggestions for friends and family need not depend upon personal confrontation. Telephoning makes distance unimportant, and we should never forget its potentialities.

Just as important is its use in local situations, where we tend to be somewhat casual. Any time we make a call, we are intruding upon someone. Usually, this intrusion is desired and necessary—but not always. As in any other confrontation, we must be sensitive to the reactions of our "host." We have to listen carefully to his voice, since we cannot see him.

Sometimes employees are hired for their voices alone. One New York executive explained that he had an English secretary just because her telephone voice was gracious and melodic. How do you think you sound?

TELEPHONE COURTESY IS IMPORTANT

Many people assume that a telephone call takes precedence over any other activity. Even normally timid people feel aggressive behind the blank mask of a telephone and forget their natural manners. What does courtesy on a telephone include?

1. Immediate identification.
2. Complete identification.
3. Making sure time is available.
4. Delivering your message first.
5. Talking directly into the mouthpiece.
6. Keeping out any extraneous noises.

177

First of all, when you call anyone, identify yourself. No matter how well you know the recipient, don't depend upon instant recognition. Extraneous noises you can't hear, preoccupation with some task, or an emotional upset can thwart recognition.

Identify yourself completely. How many Johns, Dons, Jims, Bills, Marys do you know? Give your last name. I know two Orlos. They never feel I need to know their last name. Both are Southern with deep resounding bass voices. Often, I have to fumble my way through a number of sentences before I discover who is speaking. I know they would be hurt if I asked them, "Orlo who?"

If your last name is very common or you aren't too familiar with your listener, be more specific:

"This is Bill Lee of the San Diego Bicycle Club."

Before you go any further, be sure the time is available or convenient. Most people are willing to listen for a moment or two to a quick message about a meeting time and place. For anything longer, they may ask you to call back. Others, glad to talk to you, will assure you that they have all the time in the world. You can gauge the time or amount of detailed information you should give from these clues.

Under normal circumstances, a lengthy call is questionable, no matter how much you may be reassured. Deliver the message first, in any event. If your conversation, while interesting, absorbs too much time, you may be omitted the next time you're due to have a routine call.

Some people, impervious to hints, drone on with dull voices until you are forced to be rude and virtually hang up on them. Take warning from your own reactions to a telephone hog. Keep your telephoning crisp, clear, and worth listening to. Let your warmth, your enthusiasm light up your voice.

Let that voice be properly heard by speaking directly into the mouthpiece. There are a few of us who speak too loud—not many. Let the recipient of the call adjust the distance of the earpiece in that event.

If you want to influence someone, he has to hear you. Don't waste time by mumbling into the air, inches away from the mouthpiece.

Be sure your voice is the only sound you transmit. Keep the mouthpiece below your nose. Unless we are watching a tense play, we do not want to listen to people breathing. The sound is magnified by the phone and is distracting. Sniffing, coughing, lip smacking, chewing, can all be heard. Let nothing obscure your words.

EVERYONE SHOULD KNOW HOW TO USE A TAPE RECORDER

Tapes are available on many subjects. They are effective carriers of many subjects. Some instructors and preachers automatically tape their lessons and sermons for absentees to use.

Tapes in place of letters are gaining in popularity, and rightly so. There is a warmth to them, a familiarity that pen and paper can seldom emulate, no matter how gifted the writer.

Tapes will, undoubtedly, grow in popularity as more and more people buy players and discover their versatility.

Speaking for public consumption on a tape is similar to speaking on radio. The same advantages and disadvantages apply.

For private sessions, there are one or two things to remember.

Your voice is very important. If you are very tired, put off the taping. If you are angry or worried, wait until you feel more serene.

Don't sit down ready to chat aimlessly. Have a few notes, listing the information you want to report. If the information is secret or very personal, consider where the recipient will have to listen to it. Remember, too, that anyone can pick up the tape and listen. Sometimes, private thoughts are better committed to paper than to the somewhat public medium of tape.

Generally, tapes have a vitality that cannot be surpassed. As a record of the past, they take their place. We have tapes of the voices of family members no longer with us. As we replay the tapes, a vivid picture builds and refreshes our memories. Voices are as individual and sometimes more endearing than any pictures.

Not long ago, a friend of mine wanted his brother to look at a ship he thought he would like to purchase. The brother in Australia sent the statistics through the mail, but then gave his personal opinions on tape.

The purchase looked good on paper, but after the brother's intimate personal discussion on tape, my friend decided against the transaction.

The tape was long, including many details that were unimportant, but when summed up, painted a different picture.

If you have never tried this medium, you should. It has so many advantages, and the cost is not great.

SOME PEOPLE PREFER RADIO

While radio has largely been replaced by television, there are many who prefer a medium that does not require such complete attention as television. Unfortunately, too many stations offer little more than endless hours of music, broken occasionally by weather reports and news flashes. Listeners would appreciate sensible discussions or imaginative talks. If you have an opportunity to speak on a radio program, accept it. For a beginner, it is often less terrifying than staring at people.

There are, at least, three advantages to a radio speech:

1. You may reach more people.
2. You can keep your notes available and use them constantly for reference.
3. You can be less concerned about your appearance since you are not "on view."

There are, of course, disadvantages:

1. You cannot "feel" your audience's response.

2. Your timing must be exact.
3. You must be particularly careful to avoid ambiguities.
4. You cannot open the session for questions.

Organizing your talk is the same as organizing any other, except that you must be very careful in your timing.

Most speakers write out their talks. That's fine, if you understand you are not writing an essay. The technique is quite different. More involved ideas and longer sentences can be used in written reports when an individual can go back and reread the material.

Toastmasters practice reading a talk. Unfortunately, our voices often lose spontaneity when we read. Even though you have a manuscript in front of you, you cannot "read" it. You must "tell" it.

Since the listener has no accessory means of interpretation, such as visual aids or gestures, your voice must be very clear. Precise diction matters a great deal. A monotone is out. Your voice has to perform the movement that is not visible to your audience.

Pauses are great devices with live audiences. On radio, they are important, but they must be short. The listener may feel the set is defective if there is too long a silence. A quick switch of the dial can cut off your next dramatic point.

Since no one can see you, you can use your notes without concern. You can have some marked "extra" or "can be dropped" if your timing does not come out precisely.

Microphones are extremely sensitive. Rustle your manuscript at the right moment, and your audience will hear that rather than your voice. Soft onion skin sheets are best if you plan to read. Small noises, coughs, or throat-clearing will come through loud and clear. Turn your head if a cough is inevitable. Avoid sniffling, breathing heavily, clicking teeth, or tapping a pencil. If you must underline a point, do it with your voice. Don't pound the table. That comes through like a thunderclap.

In speeches, you have one fleeting chance to present your idea. Of course, you may enlarge upon it. You may repeat it in different words, but the material should be pristine clear the first time it is presented. Since you cannot see your audience's reaction, you must be careful to make no ambiguous remarks. If you have a willing listener at home, rehearse your talk for understanding as well as timing.

Before you speak, you will ordinarily be given a voice check. Technicians are well paid to see that you can be heard properly. Let them set up the microphone. You won't need to fiddle with it, nor will you need to bend over to speak into it.

You may be given information about hand signals. Note them carefully. They will clue you in to your speed, the time left, actions that are affecting your performance. Professionals are there to help you. If anything is poor, it reflects on them. You may disagree with them, but chances are they are right in their suggestions.

How do you approach the cold, unreacting world of the microphone? You can bring along a friend or two and talk to them across the microphone. If you can't bring them along, establish them mentally before you. Radio is an intimate device. Picture their reaction to your words. A conversational tone is suitable for most talks.

You may discover you are running short of time. Be ready to omit that next-to-the-last paragraph or two. If your notes are on cards, you can drop the one marked "can be dropped." Your conclusion must be preserved and presented. You will be making your point there. The power of your thoughts must come through clearly.

On the other hand, nervousness may have sped up your speaking tempo. There are still seconds, maybe even minutes, to fill. Don't be caught short. Have on hand supplementary statistics or another anecdote or illustration that will add to your argument. These are on your "extra" cards. Presumably, you have proven your point earlier, but this is a golden opportunity to augment those statements.

In some ways, radio is a harsher medium than television. Still, anyone who has the desire to do so, can perform with clarity and understanding. He may not see the people he is talking to, but with proper preparation and presentation, he can be sure his listeners will be influenced.

18 Special Assignments Provide Opportunities to Influence

WELCOME the opportunity to take an active part in a club or committee. This is the easiest way to influence a group. Any small assignment is an opening wedge. Volunteer to lead the opening prayer or flag salute. Next, you will be asked to introduce a speaker. Finally, you will find yourself the chairman of a committee or president of the club. Speakers are willing to write their own introductions; invocations can be bought or taken from prayer books. Take a chance. Stand up before your friends or strangers and participate.

No one is likely to ask you to speak unless you have given some evidence of poise. And the way to build poise is to practice with these small but necessary parts of public programs. You can, if you are creative, add small touches that will make your performance noteworthy.

As chairman you will have to undertake to:

1. Learn the fundamentals of leadership.
2. Be firm but fair in treatment of individual members.
3. Learn and apply the Rules of Order.
4. Appoint a parliamentarian equipped with a quick reference guide to the rules.
5. Decide on a meaningful opening ceremony.
6. Prepare the audience for the speaker and the speaker for the audience.
7. Involve the members in group decisions or developments.
8. Make your reports efficient and useful.
9. Use some of the salesman's techniques.

The chairman can, with training, lead a group. Members of committees working with him can influence him.

Accept cheerfully less prominent assignments and build your influence slowly and steadily.

GUIDE A GROUP EFFECTIVELY

As chairman of a group, you'll have the spotlight on you. Share it. The role of chairman can encompass much or be severely limited—you have the choice.

If you are chairing an entire meeting, you will need to know rules of procedure. You will have to prepare an agenda, be aware of the purpose, the action to be decided, and the follow-up.

There are few leaders of groups who are not confronted with difficult situations at times, with opposition from unexpected sources. Patience, a level temper, and poise are required.

Chairmen may express their opinions if they relinquish their position temporarily. If you feel strongly enough and also think you are more informed and better able to answer penetrating questions, step down. Let your assistant chairman take over.

Generally, people want positive statements. Often, you, as chairman, will lead without being obvious. A group will respond, with relief, to a chairman's suggestion: "If there is no objection, we shall handle this matter in this way . . . "

They realize they are unaware of all the nuances and potential problems. They want leadership. If you don't lead, someone else may jump into the vacuum and inspire the group to make a less advantageous decision. Or, the matter may be tabled until the next meeting, and the same vacillation reoccurs. When you are asked to be a leader, lead.

RULES ESTABLISH LIMITS

An intelligent newly elected leader should acquaint himself quickly with the accepted methods of keeping meetings functioning efficiently. His constant concern should be to:

1. Allow less aggressive members to be heard.
2. Subdue those who are too outspoken.

The best authority is Roberts' *Rules of Order* published in New York by Scott, Foresman. It can be found in any bookstore. *Parliamentary Procedure at a Glance* by O. Garfield Jones, published by Appleton-Century-Crofts (N.Y., 1932) is a handy quick reference. This small volume, which can be carried easily, opens in the middle and is indexed so that immediate referral to a point under consideration is easily made.

Most clubs are aware of the value of a parliamentarian. If you are a leader, and there is none, make a personal appointment. If the Speaker of the House depends upon parliamentarians to provide advice when needed, you should be willing to follow his example.

If you are asked to be parliamentarian for a club, accept. This is good practice for anyone and will give you an opportunity to speak. When you do become a leader, you will find that position a lot easier.

James Madison, writing in the *Federalist,* gave a universal warning, "In all very numerous assemblies of whatever character composed, passion never fails to wrest the sceptre from reason."

Be sure you stand for reason, with a strong, comprehensive guide, in human or book form, behind you.

OPEN THE MEETING

Almost every meeting follows a traditional pattern. Flags are saluted; a monarch or president is toasted; maybe, a national anthem is sung.

The first opportunity for creativity comes with the invocation. If you are timid, you may fall back on a printed one, but even then, edit it carefully. Don't try to give a sermon. It is as important to be clear, concise, and relevant here as in any other public speech.

What religions are represented in the group? Often, the invoker calls upon his own special interpreter of God and overlooks the different beliefs. Presumably, at this time, most of us agree that there is one God. Let us restrict our supplications to Him.

Is an invocation necessary? To many, this is not a mere formality. Respect their feelings, and be sincere in your role. You know the purpose of the occasion. Try to give a meaningful invocation, one that relates the occasion to the Almighty, Who can add dimension to the event and to the awareness of the listeners. Even if the prayer is only one sentence long, practice it beforehand. There is more need to do well when you have only a short span of time.

Some organizations dispense with invocations and replace them with "thoughts for the day." Keep these, as with invocations, short and related.

Above all, speak clearly, and in an invocation, with reverence. There is no need for speed.

INTRODUCE A SPEAKER WITH FINESSE

Speakers will be more successful in a sympathetic setting. You are going to produce the right atmosphere for them. You are a means of transition from the business to the program.

Bridges should always be direct, well-structured, and, if possible, attractive. Your personality may be greater than the speaker's; however, don't try to prove it here. Focus your remarks on him. Build an interest in his work, in his individuality. But don't dwell on his subject, beyond giving positive evidences of his authority or experience in the field. That's his department.

Braude in his collection of quotations, entitled *New Treasury of Stories for Every Speaking and Writing Occasion,* says "the function of a master of ceremonies in relation to a speaker is like a fan to a dancer: it calls attention to the subject, but makes no attempt to cover it."

Norman Thomas, who toured the country and met all kinds of audiences and chairmen, said poor introducers fell into three classes. There were the ones who wanted to prove they were better speakers than he. In the second, he found chairmen who disagreed with him and wanted to provide ahead of time the antidote to the dangerous proposals they felt he was about to make. And lastly, there were those who felt they were reading his obituary; they gave all the facts and figures of his life but brushed over the subject of the talk or why they had preceded the speaker.

In capsule form, your introduction should include:

1. The subject.
2. The speaker's authority.
   a. Experience
   b. Education, if relevant
3. Honors won or successes.

188

4. Personal remark or anecdote.
5. Repeat the name clearly.

Professionals will often request that you read the information they have assembled about themselves so that you will not leave out any of what they consider the important points that constitute their authority. Reading, however, is not easy nor a particularly warm way to introduce anyone.

Be sure to collect, ahead of time, all the facts, preferably from the speaker. Use as much of them as you can, and then, if possible, insert personal information that gives another dimension to the man himself. This often makes it easier for the speaker who, from modesty, may not have given you the extra sidelights to his personality.

Beware of trite openers. Try not to say with a parrot-like chant, "It gives me great honor . . ." or, "Our guest of honor this evening needs no introduction . . ."—particularly if you are then going to talk about him for the next five minutes.

John Daly once used this introduction, but it was excusable. He said, "Ladies and gentlemen, the guest of honor this evening needs no introduction. He didn't show up."

How are you going to start if you can't use the old crutches? Use your imagination. Hook your audience:

"Tonight, we're going to hear from a man who flies kites for a living."

"Riding a bicycle across the United States is our speaker's idea of the perfect vacation."

Don't kill the speech by finishing your introduction with, "You will now hear a very interesting speech."

How can you be sure? You hope the speech will be very interesting. You may have heard it before, but every presentation is given to different listeners under different circumstances, and there are always those people who assume an "oh yeah" attitude. They immediately look for reasons to dispute anything you say. Let the speaker's speech stand on its own merits. Don't rate it ahead of time.

BUZZ SESSIONS INVOLVE THE MEMBERS

No one doubts the value of audience participation. Buzz sessions almost insure it. The large group of listeners is broken into proportionately sized smaller groups, each with a question or subject to be discussed. Their conclusions are to be reported to the others afterwards.

Experienced group leaders almost insist upon everyone speaking, voicing an opinion, or giving a suggestion. As a member of the group, you should have some ideas on the presented material. Even in this small group, the principles of public speaking are important. Make your words count. Use as few as possible, make them simple to understand, and lean heavily on positive remarks rather than critical, destructive statements. Listen to the others. Expand on their ideas. Carry them one step farther.

When it comes time to report the group's findings, volunteer. If you are selected, remember—a short, simple, but comprehensive coverage will be welcomed. Omit non-essential details and your own opinions, as such. Use notes, and refer to them to be sure you have omitted nothing. You are speaking for a group, not for yourself alone, and omission here is serious.

REPORTS MUST BE USEFUL AND CLEAR

Most working men and women are expected to report frequently to their superiors. Usually, these reports are to present information. Some carry suggestions for improvement or recommendations for the future.

When the foreman steps up to one of his bricklayers and asks, "How's it going today, Johnny?", he is asking for an informal report. The answer is usually brief and clear.

Go up the scale a bit. A report for more complicated work, done over a longer time period, and delivered in a business suit, standing before a group of executives, should be proportionately as brief and clear as Johnny's.

Determine the purpose of the report. Is it to be a summary of work completed—a progress report? Use radio and television reporters as your models. Terse, well-worded, with no hint of bias, their stories cover all the essentials.

Fact-finding surveys can be exploratory, showing potentials for future development or systematic studies of past achievements. These reports are necessarily more detailed than straight progress reports. Personal opinions may be inserted, particularly to forecast future program possibilities. Be sure the opinions are not mere prejudice but are based on research. If the suggestions are not yours, give credit to the person who developed them. Even though the group listening has a technical vocabulary, use simple, universally understood words so far as possible.

Many assigned to this sort of occupation have a fetish to be complete. Start your report from the point where you all are. Ascertain the background knowledge of the group and plunge into fresh information as quickly as you can. Stick to your material. Don't ramble. Remember you may be willing to waste five minutes of your time, but you are also wasting five minutes of theirs. Multiply that by the number of listeners you have. Then consider the average salary they are receiving while listening to you. Have you the temerity to cost that much? Be sure you give value for money and time expended.

This is one time when careful preparation and efficient presentation invariably influence the listeners.

SALESMEN HAVE A SPECIAL APPROACH

Over the years, salesmen have carefully researched the subject of how to influence their customers to buy. We can learn from them.

Primarily, they have five guide rules:

1. Arouse the customer's interest by complimenting him about something personal.
2. Introduce the product or service with a positive statement, relating it to the customer.

3. Make statements with which the customer must agree because of the obvious truth or because the customer's ego is involved.
4. Use words that are soothing, not frightening.
5. Phrase questions that cannot be answered with a definite "no."

Most of these rules can be employed in public speaking.

Here is an example of instructions given to new real estate salesmen in one office in California:

Words are important. "Buy" connotes spending money, which frightens would-be purchasers. "Making an investment," however, is a "wise move." You never "buy a lot." You "make an investment in land."

Never ask a major question that can be answered with a definite "no." That will automatically shut off any further persuading. For example, don't ask baldly, "Would you be interested in purchasing this lot?" Ask instead, "How much insurance would you like to carry on this property?"

During the presentation, be willing to listen to objections. Objections indicate interest. After the protest has been made, repeat the objection, look a little defeated, then say, "Let me see if I understand your question or objection."

When the objection is confirmed, say, "You mean that's the only objection you have?"

Question the objection, "Tell me why you feel it's important, or why it's a question."

In the course of this discussion, the prospect may talk himself out of the objection. If all else fails, however, answer the question.

If a sale is about to be consummated, do not say, "Sign here."

Instead, offer a pen. "Use my ballpoint, why don't you?" Or say, "Shall we wrap it up now?"

As you see, there is no dishonesty in any of these statements. They have, however, been chosen for their subtle effects on the listeners.

If you are interested in the subject, read James K. Van Fleet's book entitled *How to Put Yourself Across with People*

(Parker Publishing Co., Inc., 1971) 228 pp. The material is not only interesting, but also it is applicable in every situation.

Public speakers should consider the techniques, although they may be speaking to a larger group. They can influence or impress by careful word choice or approach to a contentious idea. What do *you* want to sell to your audience?

19

Influence Many at Conventions

CONVENTIONS attract the thinkers, the doers, the outgoing. Can you think of a better place to meet people willing to be influenced? The opportunities are manifold. You can learn as well as observe leaders at work, influencing others to do as they do.

Influence and be influenced to do better. Professional societies vie with skilled workers, hobbyists, religious groups, sports enthusiasts, and political parties for space in congenial surroundings where many lines of cooperative activities can be followed.

Where do you fit in?

1. Conventions in your area need speakers:
   a. To set up the convention.

b. To discuss the subject matter.
c. To discuss related subject matter.
d. To welcome and present possible extracurricular diversions.
e. To sum up decisions for absentees.
2. Out-of-town conventions need speakers:
   a. To develop interest for potential attenders before the meeting.
   b. To present papers.
   c. To demonstrate sales products.
   d. To make reports for absentees after the meeting.

You can begin your apprenticeship by serving in a different capacity than speaking: alerting other members by phone, making signs, mailing out information. As you become more self-confident, you can proceed into the speaking end.

Perhaps your organizational activities will catch the eye of a Board member, and you will be recommended for a national committee. You may even decide to volunteer to present a paper.

My first assignment at a national convention was as a member of the program committee. We reviewed proposed papers and made recommendations concerning them to the Convention Chairman for the Institute of Environmental Engineers. As an immediate result, I was nominated and elected Vice-President-Publications for the national society. I worked with men who were active and outstanding in my own field. For a number of years thereafter, I was approached by executives from aerospace firms throughout the country offering me positions.

Conventions, today, are vital. They gather together people from many areas, with new ideas. Those who come want to hear what you have to say, personally or on the platform. If conventions are held nearby, volunteer to make them more meaningful—if not for others, for yourself.

If those in your field are scheduled elsewhere, make an effort to attend. Your company may pay your way. If not, go on your own. A vacation is a change of pace from a regular pursuit. You may find your pace so changed, you can never again march to the same old music. You may find your ideas so accepted that your influence will be greater, longer, and farther-reaching than you can possibly imagine.

HOME-TOWN CONVENTIONS ARE GREAT OPPORTUNITIES

A convention requires an untold number of workers. You will have no problem finding a niche where you can serve. To locate the one most desirable to you, start early.

At one time, convention sites were chosen a year in advance. No more. With the tremendous development of transportation and the willingness of people to travel great distances, the more attractive places are often reserved five or six years in advance.

Be aware of the schedules of your special organizations. Volunteer at a convention prior to the one to be held in your town. Ask the chairmen of former conventions about their problems and successes. They're eager to tell about the pitfalls they have either fallen into or avoided.

You can offer to handle administrative details. Even more, you can speak on a one-to-one basis to stimulate attendance. If the convention is a large one, encompassing a number of clubs, you can appear before them, influencing them to attend. Make the convention a success before it begins.

The obvious offering would be to speak, to present a paper or chairman a panel of experienced members. Volunteer! Make suggestions to the program committee! Your ideas may influence their planning even though your suggestions are not accepted in exactly the same format.

You can welcome the visitors. That's usually the job of the host chairman or national president or mayor. But there are allied groups connected with each larger group: wives, or teenagers, or teachers at general church conventions, husbands at women's conventions.

Someone has to point out the interesting features of the

area, arrange for speakers from local tourist attractions, research institutes, or manufacturing specialties.

In our town, the tuna industry is featured. We have a world-famous, fairly unique school, Scripps Institute of Oceanography. We have special gardening opportunities, and so on. What does your town offer that's different?

Attend the meetings that are helpful to you. Absorb the information so that you can present it to those unable to be there. Be ready to sum up decisions that can be helpful to your group or company.

CONVENTIONS IN OTHER FIELDS WELCOME SPEAKERS

Expand your involvement beyond your own field of interest. Perhaps you have a message that can add significance to other conventions that meet in your town. Chambers of commerce or convention bureaus know long in advance which groups are planning to meet. The different program chairmen are often willing to add a speaker who has something to say, particularly when they don't have to pay travel and hotel expenses.

I had one of my most interesting experiences when I was asked to address the International Turf Grass Conference. This group is responsible for the care and maintenance of golf courses here and abroad. How far removed from aerospace could I get? After hours, my sport is bicycling. My few attempts at golf were almost disastrous.

Two thousand people registered for the convention. More than 600 attended the talk I gave about Toastmasters and their self-help program. The convention chairman had initiated the subject, writing to the San Diego Tourist and Convention Bureau. As the current governor of the Toastmasters in the district, my name was listed with them.

Register yourself as a potential speaker at any local bureau. Write to the headquarters of organizations scheduling meetings. Suggest your participation. You may even collect a fee! Programs, ordinarily, are planned by a headquarters staff. With an eye to the budget, they are happy to entertain the idea of using local talent that is appropriate.

What specialty do you have that could appeal to a wide range of visitors? Gather your material. Send out a few queries. If possible, give them a list of places where you have spoken and references. The worst they can do is say, "no, thank you"—and by mail! You don't have to face them unless they are truly interested. Half the battle is won.

OUT-OF-TOWN CONVENTIONS ARE GREAT OPPORTUNITIES

Maybe you live in a remote area, and none of the large conventions come to your town. Then, go to them. No matter how much research you do, you cannot reach the levels of inspiration you get from meeting alert leaders who are bursting with enthusiasm and advanced know-how.

Enduring friendships are based on like interests discovered during the annual week of meetings carried on in different areas of the country. All kinds of opportunities open up to people who are exposed to them. Go to these conventions for your vocation, your hobby, your church. You will grow. Your mind will be stimulated. You will be exposed to opportunities. You will have the opportunity to influence others.

If the expenses seem enormous, and you feel the cost is too great, watch for the call for papers. Engineers are not noted for their interest in lectures, yet I found a fertile field. Your company, if it is progressive, will be delighted to add to its reputation by having representation at a professional gathering. Most companies will pay your way.

Do you think you're not outstanding enough? Most of the speakers are not nationally or internationally known. Let me give you an idea of the number of speakers needed at one three-day convention, held by the Institute of Environmental Engineers. There were 354 men delivering papers or acting as chairmen or panel moderators for the five sessions which met concurrently every day. Twenty-five specialists gave lectures during teaching seminars as part of the educational program. Eighty-two environmental equipment manufacturers held special sessions during a service-and-maintenance clinic. There were 461 speeches in the formal events!

Also, add to this the talks given in committee meetings prior to the convention, the appeals at the local chapters urging attendance, sales pitches, final reports after the event, and the all-important resumés for the ones who were unable to be there. With so much talk going on, you certainly have many opportunities for speaking and influencing.

CONVENTION SPEAKERS HAVE BUILT-IN REQUIREMENTS

Speakers at conventions have a few special considerations—ones that were important in other situations but are magnified in these circumstances.

1. Timing is vital and frequently changed at the last minute.
2. Many speeches are written out beforehand and published.
3. Questioning sessions are usually expected.

Time is very important. You are assigned a special slot that must fit into an overall program. Arriving late or taking a casual extra ten minutes may throw off the next speaker. The whole program may be jeopardized because of you. Be flexible enough so that you can either expand or condense your material if you're on the receiving end of the mismanaged time. Often, schedules have to be revised at the last minute. The chairman may have to slip another speaker into your session, requesting you to cut ten minutes off your talk.

Sometimes, a speaker does not appear, and you are asked to expand your talk to fill the allotted time. In one of the sessions I attended, the chairman set up the other speaker and me as a two-man panel and extended the question period.

Ordinarily, your speech will have to be written. Most major professional conventions publish proceedings which include the talks. Some hand out the speeches before you make them. While you are not expected to read your paper, you had better stick to it fairly closely. Why speak at all? Many prefer to hear the talk, using the printed pages as notes or report material for the stay-at-homes.

Present the key features in a conversational manner. Look at your audience and make them aware that you are talking to them as individuals. Beyond the subject matter, you can add the reasons why you became involved in this specific aspect, and how, when, and where you performed this particular task or experiment. Most important, tell how the subject is applicable or can help them in their work.

Whenever possible, reserve time for questions. This is often the greatest challenge in your session. If you are well-versed in your subject, you can be of great service offering solutions to problems. You may make someone's trip worthwhile. Hours of research may be eliminated. He won't forget you!

Remember, too, you are competing with others in your field if simultaneous sessions are held. You want to build a reputation that will make your colleagues choose your session first, because they know you center your talk on them and their problems. You never waste time, and you make your speech vital and interesting.

What happier feeling can you have than to realize that because of you professionals from Maine to California, and some abroad, are working more effectively? You showed them the way. You influenced them.

WIDEN YOUR BASE WITH A VARIETY OF INTERESTS

We have stressed professional and vocational conferences because an individual's work consumes the greatest number of his hours. But a whole person is made up of many parts, and his interests should be diverse.

What are your side interests? Attend conventions centered on those fields. Robert Higgins, an engineer, became so engrossed in model railroading that he developed a second income presenting papers and reports to meetings and journals on this hobby. It was started for fun, but with recurring economic upheavals, that "second string" may become all-important.

Keep an open mind as you live from day to day. An unexpected spot of information can develop into a full-time avocation or occupation. It's like any other subject—people and communication open the way to a more meaningful future.

Where do you find the greatest number of like-minded people? At a convention. Seek them out for inspiration. Listen well. Then, add your own special slant. You will attract alert individuals, and your influence will make itself felt in unexpected places.

Section VI

**THE ROAD
TO SUCCESS**

20

Start Today
to Build Your Power
to Influence

No matter what day it is, the time to begin is now. Ripping up irritating material that comes through the mail, grousing at your family because of the high cost of living, deploring silently that none of the candidates is any good, is a futile way to live.

Think seriously about a better solution. Investigate all the plans offered. Study the ideas and platforms of promoters or candidates. Then, if you have something to offer, speak out. If you feel one program or candidate deserves support, tell people—a small group or a large one. Tell them why, using the principles that have been outlined in these chapters.

Most people are influenced by someone who has apparently taken the time and made the effort to discover a better way of life. Be careful, however, to deserve their trust. It may seem to take forever to win men's minds by persuasion, but it is quicker than doing it by force—and, it lasts!

Having once been accepted as a thinker, you will be surprised to discover that you are considered an expert in many unrelated fields.

SET GOALS FOR YOURSELF

Few reach the end of a journey in one jump. Map your way to your destination, and travel that first mile today.

Most of us bumble along life's pathway, pushed by immediate needs, our eyes upon the "now" road. Skiers who concentrate on what's underfoot, invariably fall. Their gaze must be centered yards ahead. So it is in life. Live day by day, but keep your eyes focussed on your objectives a month, a year, a decade ahead.

"He who builds no castles in the air, builds no castles anywhere." The unknown author of this axiom gives us a valuable tip.

Picture yourself in the position you would like to attain. Accept the idea that you will be there some day, that the capabilities of being there are latent within you. All you need to do is uncover them and work at your desire.

SUCCESS DEPENDS UPON COMMUNICATION

Communicating may be the first rung on any ladder to success. Early training in good speech patterns is something over which you have no control. You may have to back-track to be sure your grammar is adequate. Sloppy diction or traces of dialect may have to be overcome. No one can correct these for you. But, on the other hand, no one can prevent you from improving yourself.

Physical speech defects may seem an insurmountable

barrier, but if all else is right, many of them will be overlooked. One of the highest-paid professional speakers today has a severe speech defect. Her first five sentences are shockers while her listeners absorb the fact that she has a problem.

After that interval, her manner of presentation, her charming personality, and her material are all that matters. You can follow her example. Lose yourself in your enthusiasm for your subjects, and your audience will respond.

Don't lay this book down and say to yourself that some day you will do something about it. Right now, find a pencil and set down the goals you wish to reach. Determine the path you must follow.

CHECK YOUR COMMUNICATION SKILLS

Consider first your voice.

1. Do you speak clearly, giving each word its proper value? Mumbling, dragging out vowel sounds, or speaking too quickly makes listening difficult. Women frequently pitch their voices too high, or let them ascend as they speak, until the result is almost a whine.

2. Do you speak in a monotone or in breathy word clumps? Is your voice too soft, or do people cringe from the harshness or power of your voice?

Your second investigation should center on your language.

1. Has slang always seemed colorful to you? How up-to-date are those words or phrases that punctuate your speech? Do you honestly believe that being "with it" in terms of unorthodox language will impress your listeners? Nothing succeeds as well as understandable, conventional words.

2. Are you too impressed with big words? I was once told that almost every word in the dictionary has a different meaning. The difference may be infinitesimal, but it is there, and only the exact word should be used. Not so! It is better to use five short words than five-syllable tongue-twisters most of the time. Use your discretion. Many highly educated citizens are edu-

cated only within a specific field, and that did not include a language with its intricate variations and nuances of meaning.

GATHER MATERIAL AND EXPERIENCE

When you have mastered the technicalities, study your subject thoroughly. Using the research books mentioned in earlier chapters, learn everything you can. Keep a file of notes. Begin a joke collection. Gather apt quotations.

Try a session or two at home with friends, leading them in discussions from the Great Books series, the Foreign Policy Association's Great Decisions, or any subject of interest. Invite your neighbors to a political "coffee" if you feel a candidate or a proposition is worthwhile.

Go further afield when you feel confident. Offer yourself to speakers' bureaus for local issues, bond drives, the United Community Services. Scout leaders are always willing to open their meetings to speakers on snake bites, traffic safety, bike riding. Senior citizens' clubs, service organizations, YMCAs, and the USO are great opportunities for you to meet, to talk, to influence.

Every time you help others, you are accumulating a wealth of experience for yourself. Your poise under every condition will improve, and your wits will sharpen.

The view from the top of the ladder may be delightful, but it can be reached only one step at a time. Set your goals. But most of all, take that first step *now!*

BUILD YOUR SELF-IMAGE

What do you really think of yourself? Do you project an image of self-confidence and assurance? Or are you hesitant?

Most of us have much to be hesitant about, everyone agrees. The converse is just as true. Most of us have much to be proud of. Make a list of your good qualities. You won't have to flaunt it. This is for yourself.

Ask your family what they think are your best traits. If you have a close friend or two, you can ask them. Recall what your superior has said about you in his last performance review. You may be surprised to discover qualities which you have not considered important.

Concentrate on your strengths. Build out from them. You already know some of your more annoying habits. Try to eliminate or soften them. But don't concentrate on elimination—work positively.

You may be proud of your strength when it comes to "speaking out" about shoddy work or weak excuses. Can you handle a situation like this without destructive results? Saving face for someone, helping to stimulate a lazy or disrespectful person to more helpful ways, is the better way. As you pull others up to a more attractive self-image, your own image grows.

You have begun well when you develop your effectiveness as a speaker. A colleague, a supervisor will listen to you if you have something to offer.

You will be the first to realize if your contribution is not worthwhile. You lower yourself in your own mind. And the effect is contagious. Be proud of your work. Communicate with those around you in the spirit of cooperation, comprehension, and progress, and your influence cannot help but grow.

TOASTMASTERS INTERNATIONAL DEVELOPS LEADERS

You are not alone in your search for dynamic personality growth. More than a million men have improved their speaking abilities and become leaders. More than 70,000 each year openly practice and learn through Toastmasters International.

Toastmasters feel membership in their organization can:

1. Help you become an effective speaker.
2. Teach you careful listening.
3. Teach you critical thinking.

4. Prepare you for conducting or participating in meetings.
5. Develop your leadership abilities.
6. Provide you with enjoyable fellowship and a forum for a stimulating interchange of ideas.

You can practice and try out your skills on your own. Many are successful. Many have a natural ability to speak, to sway audiences. William Jennings Bryan knew he had this ability although he had no idea of why he was so persuasive.

You can save yourself a lot of time by joining a Toastmasters Club. There are, at this writing, 3,400 clubs in 47 countries. Their stated purpose is to develop leadership through communication. Their slogan—*better thinking, better listening, better speaking*—is not a casual choice.

Every meeting gives every member a chance to participate. Assigned speeches, lasting from five to seven minutes each, are the highlights of each session, but everyone present is expected to speak.

Part of the meeting is set aside for Table Topics. Members, not already assigned to some speaking part in the program, talk from one to two minutes on a subject assigned by a Topicmaster. No one has more than two minutes of preparation. The subjects range from trivia to serious problems of the community, nation, or world.

This is excellent training for the man who has always hesitated to put forth his opinions. He has little time to worry about inconsequentials; he has no time to ramble because a bell cuts him off when his time is up.

New members are always asked to speak about themselves for five minutes as an "ice breaker" speech. Almost everyone is sure he cannot talk that long. Almost everyone is shocked to discover how soon his time limit is reached.

A carefully prepared manual outlines various points of emphasis: The Well-Constructed Speech; How to Make Words Work for You; How to Be More Persuasive. There are 15 basic speech projects.

A second volume develops more advanced procedures,

such as the book review, after-dinner speaking, and written speeches.

Most members take about two or three years to cover the assignments, but they have other opportunities as they are learning, to participate in speakers' bureaus, which most districts have established.

EVALUATION BUILDS EFFECTIVENESS

Most important, to my mind, is the evaluation session. Major speakers have individual evaluators who assess each talk according to specific points. The informal Table Topics are evaluated on a general basis. Often, a trophy for the most effective weekly speaker in each segment travels between members.

Don Paape, an elected officer of Toastmasters International, is an enthusiastic supporter of careful evaluations. He says, "Unless each of us provides our fellow club members with specific means and methods of improving their communication abilities, we lose interest and the desire to improve."

Evaluations are made in the spirit of goodwill and are accepted as such. Praising without deserving calls for a "whitewash brush," which both the evaluator and the speaker aim to avoid.

For this service alone, a club membership is invaluable. Where else can you find an unbiased, intelligent, helpful critique?

LEADERSHIP TRAINING FOR EVERYONE

Above and beyond the public speaking experience is leadership training. Ordinarily, in each club, top officers hold their positions for only one term, to give more members experience in conducting meetings Toastmasters consider all this as part of their learning experience. Unlike most organizations, the offices are eagerly sought. Campaigns with speeches of support are part of the f n and training.

Meetings are usually run conventionally, with frequent referral to Roberts' *Rules of Order.* As the chairman becomes more experienced, the members provide him with innovative motions. Hecklers take over. Arguments break out on the floor. No chairman can escape a thorough grounding in how to handle almost any situation in accordance with accepted standards.

For the women, Toastmistress Clubs present the same sort of self-help program.

WHERE YOU CAN FIND HELP

Check your telephone book. Many local groups of Toastmasters and Toastmistresses have a general information number. Chambers of Commerce list the clubs that meet in their area.

If you cannot locate one, the general headquarters will be glad to send you the information:

- Toastmasters International World Headquarters
  220 North Grand Avenue
  Santa Ana, California 92711
- International Toastmistress Clubs, Inc.
  9068 East Firestone Boulevard, Suite 2
  Downey, California 90241

Large companies and management clubs frequently subsidize membership costs or provide meeting places or both, realizing that improvement on the part of any employee upgrades the corporation.

If no club now exists, perhaps you should take the initiative and establish one.

Whatever you do, the time is here. Take that first step, *now!*

THIS IS SUCCESS

The expectant hush of a waiting audience is a living, almost-tangible aura. The hum of agreement, responsive chuckles, sympathetic stirrings, applause of appreciation or approval are value indeed for the work you will do, the effort you will make to communicate.

This is success—to touch men's hearts and minds; to stimulate; to amuse; to inform; to influence others to better ways or happier lives. There are few greater pleasures.